DOWRY
OF A
NOBODY

flea market style

flea market style

Emily Chalmers   *with words by Ali Hanan*

photography by Debi Treloar

RYLAND
PETERS
& SMALL

LONDON NEW YORK

First published in
the UK in 2005 by
Ryland Peters & Small
20-21 Jockey's Fields
London WC1R 4BW
www.rylandpeters.com

10 9 8 7 6 5 4 3 2

ISBN 978 1 84172 937 4

A CIP record for this book is
available from the British Library.

Printed and bound in China.

SENIOR DESIGNER Paul Tilby
SENIOR EDITOR Henrietta Heald
LOCATION RESEARCH Emily Chalmers
and Emily Westlake
PRODUCTION Patricia Harrington
ART DIRECTOR Gabriella Le Grazie
PUBLISHING DIRECTOR Alison Starling

contents

introduction

I magine. It's a Saturday morning. Rather than heading to the high street, you have strolled to a local market. Each stall brims with gems. In among the bric-à-brac are vintage fabrics, polished silver cutlery, fine bone-china teacups, and look! – there's a diamond – a nut-brown leather club chair complete with its original soft velvet cushion.

Sigh. If only your wicker shopping bag were a hundred times larger and came with wheels and an engine. High-street buys pale beside second-hand pieces with colourful past lives. What's more, market pieces survive because they were built for years of service. Old-timers such as copper pots, heirloom linens, mahogany rolltop desks and cast-iron kettles have done their time – and lived to tell the tale. Some finds

were also created with an artistry increasingly rare and precious in an age of mass-production. The tiny errant line on a hand-painted roll of wallpaper or a thumb print on a hand-made vase gives these pieces a twist of humanity.

Beautiful things never go out of style. Classics endure. And, if it's your lucky day, you may even bag a real jewel, like an original Eames chair or a swooping Castiglioni 'Swan' lamp, which you can snap up for a song. Pieces like this retain – and even increase – their value.

Some pieces will be welcomed as they are but others will need tender loving care or urgent cosmetic surgery. Choose a piece if it has promise. If a sofa with good bone structure needs a facelift, for example, simply fashion a cover for it out of a vintage fabric. Other pieces can be resuscitated and reinvented. Dress up a Cinderella cushion with an antique brooch or give a Plain Jane lampshade

a gorgeous new gown made from old ribbons. Once you are a seasoned talent scout, you will be able to see a piece's potential and dream up a whole new career for it, like using a bench as a side table or a chipped teacup as a dainty vase.

Dip into the first part of the book, Flea Market Finds, to see what's on offer at second-hand stalls. Whether your style is retro, minimalist, rock-'n'-roll or eclectic, you will see how to choose furniture, kitchenware, lighting and fabrics to suit it. Putting It All Together shows you how to transform your interior, room by room. The book ends with ideas on where to source finds. Apart from markets, items are also commonly spotted at jumble sales, village fairs and auctions, in rubbish skips and on internet sites.

Be inspired. Turn the pages and discover what kind of orphaned finds you can adopt and bring home to a new life. Shun the consumerism of the high street. Recycle and revive pieces with soul and style – and you will be able to create a loved, lived-in space that you can really call home.

flea market finds

Old chairs, tables, beds, bookcases, desks, drawers, sofas, armchairs, stools and wardrobes come in all shapes, sizes and styles – and can often be picked up for a song. Choose pieces to suit your taste – or create your own eclectic look.

furniture

A home furnished with second-hand pieces seems more lived-in and loved than one furnished mostly with new items. Unlike hot-off-the-shop-floor high-street products, second-hand things have a casual, careworn air. Some found objects have their own quirks; some need a bit of mending – but give any item a little tender loving care or a fresh twist and watch it blossom into new life.

What's more, market-found furniture comes in an enormous range of decorative styles. Timeless pieces, such as old leather sofas and refectory tables, have an important feature in common with faded denim jeans and little black dresses: they always look good. For urban loft dwellers, there are pieces to suit the raw, hard edges of industrial chic (think old dental chairs, office swivel seats, filing cabinets). For those who hanker after the soft, rustic looks of country style, many markets have whole fields of furniture ripe for harvesting (think wicker storage baskets, wooden rocking chairs, farmhouse-style tables). If your taste is retro, you will find a feast of vintage furniture, including

ABOVE Who would have imagined that this lovely lady in red would need to be rescued from a skip? She now looks stunning in a vibrant scarf, fashioned into a cushion cover.

OPPOSITE Many once-loved pieces need a simple makeover. For example, a set of drawers that came from an office looks pretty in a coat of pink paint.

Think of yourself as a talent scout seeking supermodels. You will quickly learn how to spot a gorgeous piece at a hundred paces.

wooden sideboards, kidney-shaped tables and low-level vinyl sofas. Whatever your style, there will always be something to satisfy the magpie instinct.

While you are bound to find something to suit your taste, you will also find classics at affordable prices. Buying brand-new high-quality pieces is very expensive, but if you buy new low-cost furniture the choice is mainly restricted to flat-packed items, which tend to push a self-destruct button after only a few months of use. If you bone up on design classics, you could unearth a coveted gem such as an original Verner Panton 'S' chair or a Charles and Ray Eames recliner. Such treasures will retain or even increase their value if kept in mint condition, so when it comes to reselling them you could be (literally) sitting on a small fortune.

When it comes to buying furniture, think of yourself as a talent scout searching for potential supermodels. You will quickly learn how to spot a gorgeous piece at a hundred paces. Start by checking for sound bone structure and chose one with a sturdy, hardy frame, springs and legs, and intact stuffing. If the piece of furniture is in good shape but looks haggard, think cosmetic surgery. It is easy to give furniture a facelift with a new coat of paint, a new cover or a little artful customizing. Try furniture out before you buy it, since looks can be deceptive (you don't want a spring sticking into your back when you're reading the Sunday papers).

THIS PAGE Let an old
sofa step out in style in
a new dress; this one has
had its ageing white cover
dyed a refreshing blue.

OPPOSITE, ABOVE
Hallways are frequently no
more than traffic routes,
but with a hip find such as
this retro chair, you won't
want to just walk on by.

OPPOSITE, BELOW
LEFT A luxurious red
leather sofa has had its
sassy looks softened by a
floral cushion sewn from
an old kitchen curtain.

OPPOSITE, BELOW
RIGHT This 'Swan' chair
by Danish designer Arne
Jacobsen was discovered
at a Copenhagen market.

THIS PAGE An antique, gilt-edged console found at London's Portobello market gives a modern space an air of old-fashioned luxury. Adorning its smooth top is an oriental-style glass tree plucked from a car-boot sale, now used to display its owner's jewellery. The print above is a common, but classic, art find.

Some found objects have quirks; some need mending – but give any item a little tender loving care or a fresh twist and watch it blossom into new life.

Seating is an essential element of virtually every space in the home, especially the living room. When it comes to armchairs and sofas, watch out for signs of use such as shiny patches on arms or saggy seating. Those details show that the seat is comfortable enough to have been sat on for hours in the past. One thing that seems to appeal to all tastes is the come-hither warmth of a loved leather sofa. Other fabric-covered pieces may be found in great shape but with a dated 'dress', so re-upholster them in a new or vintage fabric. For an instant new cover, drape an old bedspread, checked blanket or

faux fur throw over the sofa. Or add *va-va-vroom* with cushions fashioned from vintage fabrics and adorned with brooches, ribbons or buttons.

While sofas and armchairs are at home in living rooms, so too are pieces like chaises-longues and daybeds. Old chaise-longues often bring with them an air of elegance and grandeur. If quirky modern is your style, make an old-world chaise-longue more funky by re-upholstering it with a zebra print cover; if you're a classicist, complement its antique charm with embroidered silk cushions. These pieces look seductive in a bedroom or decadent in a bathroom.

ABOVE LEFT Bring old pieces into rooms for which they were not originally intended. Repainted in a crisp white, this chest of drawers is at home in a minimalist-style living room.

ABOVE A sideboard from the 1960s is used for both storage and display. The 'paint by numbers' picture above it was inspired by a vintage silk scarf pattern.

therapists' chairs, bar stools, architects' chairs, laboratory stools and office chairs. Your finds may need a little paintwork here or a new cover there, but they will introduce into your home elements that are slightly eccentric and fabulously original.

You may find it hard to find a complete set of dining chairs, so cherry-pick individual chairs with a common theme (fold-out garden chairs, wooden café chairs or 1960s chairs) to create harmony – or go eclectic and create an array of mismatching chairs, softening hard edges and giving a sense of 'family' with a range of matching cushions.

When it comes to tables, aficionados can choose from second-hand office desks, old garden tables,

A daybed is easy to make (simply shorten the legs of a small single bed) and is usually handier than a pull-out sofa for overnight guests. Create a backrest of multicoloured cushions for daytime use.

Another junk find that's often dismissed is the bench (think old church pews or school-assembly benches). Often made from best-quality wood, a bench can double as a table or as overflow seating for dinner parties. To make it comfortable, simply fashion some squab cushions from vintage fabrics.

The choice of chairs is as endless as the way in which they can be used. Seek out old wrought-iron chairs, ex-café chairs, metal stools, rocking chairs and wicker chairs for every room, but also think laterally, bringing home retired 'working' chairs such as dentists' chairs, old cinema seats, massage

THIS PAGE A handsome cabinet with sliding doors offers generous storage for all sorts of recycled boxes housing odds and ends.

OPPOSITE, LEFT A piece of salvaged netting divides this living space into zones. The chair is an electric massage chair; originally clad in vinyl, it has been stripped down and re-upholstered in floral fabrics for a softer look.

OPPOSITE, RIGHT Outdoor pieces can work well indoors; this former wire-mesh plant rack has been reinvented as a shelf for books and ornaments.

THIS PAGE AND
OPPOSITE Be inventive,
like the owner of this house,
who has jazzed up pieces
of furniture with a thick
coat of blackboard paint.
She has chalked her son's
name all over his chest of
drawers and adorned the
hall cupboard with poetry
in a flowing, looping hand.
These furniture sculptures
are thrown into relief by a
canvas of pale-grey walls.

THIS PAGE Markets offer many storage pieces such as the chests below (left and right); customize them with brightly hued paints. A set of mirrors in various shapes (below left) does the same job on a wall as a single long mirror.

OPPOSITE Once used to store household linens, this old wardrobe now houses a collection of crockery. Beside it is a found sofa, which demonstrates how a chintzy, kitsch piece can appear lustrous when set against a plain canvas.

bedside tables and pine refectory tables. The list is endless. If you have enough space, look for one of the many farmhouse-style pine tables that turn up at furniture markets; if you don't have much space, alternatives include tables with drop leaves or extendable tables to accommodate surplus guests. Then there is always the ultimate junk-find table: a sanded door or a large piece of heavy glass mounted on a pair of reclaimed trestles; just cover it with a beautiful cloth to hide its haphazard look.

You will find many retro kidney tables or bent-chrome-and-glass 1970s tables to serve as coffee tables. As for bedside tables, the choice depends on how inventive you are. Tables big enough for a couple of books, a reading light and a water jug are easily fashioned out of small wooden stools, old school desks or folding butler's tray tables.

Wooden tea trolleys make equally useful kitchen storage. Alternatively, you can sever the trolley's legs to make an instant side table or children's dining table. Many former work tables such as office desks, architects' drawing boards and sewing tables can be converted into home-office desks.

Efficient storage is an essential element of any home. Chests of drawers, side cabinets, wardrobes, bookcases, plate racks and cupboards – in all shapes and sizes – turn up regularly at second-hand outlets and in a huge range of styles.

All you need to do to update them is to sand them and give them a fresh, thick coat of paint, or paper the doors with vintage wallpaper. Or you could customize drawers with funky new handles (fashion a handle out of old rope or thick ribbon or use vintage door handles). Old tea chests, beautiful antique leather suitcases, toy chests, big wicker baskets, old laundry baskets and wine boxes also create covetable storage.

One easy way to introduce pattern, colour and texture into a Cinderella interior is with textiles. Every market or second-hand shop is a treasure trove of curtains, quilts, lace, shawls, tea towels and end-cuts of fabric bolts – in a wide range of weights, qualities and patterns. Another solution is the clever use of junk-find wallpapers.

pattern and colour

OPPOSITE A boldly striped pillow and throw have been used to update an old sofa, whose arms fold down to create a daybed. A patchwork of wallpaper samples adorns the wall behind it.

ABOVE RIGHT Don't judge a chair by its cover. If you like the shape of a chair but not its garb, simply have it re-upholstered.

Observe how easily something ordinary can become extraordinary through the addition of pattern and colour from fabrics, wallpapers or paints. Imagine covering a plain wall with a patchwork of wallpaper samples. Or visualize a minimalist bedroom with a wrought-iron bed covered in a stark white bedcover and an old wardrobe in the corner. Garnish the bed with one colourful cushion and somehow the whole room is transformed. It is softer. It has a centre. That is the quiet power of pattern and colour.

When you use pattern, remember that a little goes a long way. Pattern draws the eye, becoming a focal point, so mix it with plenty of large plain areas. If you want your busy, chintzy sofa to be your living room's exclamation mark, keep the backdrop plain. Conversely, if you have discovered a roll of graphically decorated 1970s wallpaper, ensure that the sofa in front of it is neutral.

Colour schemes usually work best when devised in one of three ways: either by using contrasting colours (for example, red teamed with blue, or turquoise with orange); or by using complementary tones of the same colour (for example, khaki, sage and lime green, or cobalt blue, azure and sky blue); or by combining harmonious colours (for example, ruby red and orange, or chocolate and violet).

Ideas for decorative schemes have many sources. You could base your colour palette on a find such as a roll of vintage floral wallpaper, a red leather sofa or a beautiful orange vase, or you might prefer to search for accessories once you have chosen your favourite paint colour as a backdrop. A fresh green, for example, may prompt you to track down natural or naturally inspired objects to accompany it, such as a nut-brown leather sofa, a wooden-framed mirror or a large leafy plant in a terracotta pot.

Remember that light colours make small spaces appear bigger, while dark colours make walls feel closer. If you want to alter the way your space is perceived, apply these rules by bringing colour, pattern and texture into the floor and walls – your interior's largest canvases.

ABOVE Stack patterned fabric finds to create small piles of visual interest.

OPPOSITE Just as you might do with an outfit, you can crown your sofa or bed with a chic accessory. Here, a trio of cushions made from vintage scarves turn heads on a bed.

THIS PAGE Soften the hard edges of wooden chairs with cushions. This foursome was created from various floral finds. Being fashioned from fabrics with a related colour theme makes them into a set.

LEFT This beautiful fabric length, used as a curtain to inhibit cold draughts, is like an artwork in itself. The hard look of the door, covered in blackboard paint, is instantly softened with a white lace curtain.

RIGHT Held in place by pebbles from the sea shore, a floral scarf makes a translucent window blind.

Avoid visual mayhem by papering a single wall and painting the room's other walls in a neutral colour.

LEFT Use finds to create screens and drapes that dare to be different. This striking patchwork of silk scarves, all loosely tacked together, offsets the hard-edged feel of a former warehouse. An old metal postal cabinet is home to piles of fabric finds, all waiting to be used.

Second-hand wall-hangings and wallpaper are ideal for revitalizing your space. Unpopular in the 1990s – when white paint splashed its way over countless interior walls – wallpaper is now making a comeback. With it comes colour, pattern and, in some cases, texture. Second-hand markets offer a range of vintage papers. Visual mayhem can easily be avoided by papering a single wall and painting the other walls in a neutral colour. Sometimes you will find insufficient wallpaper to cover the whole wall. If this happens, look for a complementary paper and paper the wall in alternating stripes.

Some wallpaper patterns are overpowering, but, if you are passionate about a particular design or find a beautiful piece of wrapping paper, use it to jazz up other surface areas, such as storage boxes, files, wardrobe doors, bedheads and built-in bath exteriors. Old hand-painted papers are sometimes masterpieces in their own right. Turn them into display items by inserting a cutting into a big wooden frame or papering a wrap-around canvas.

When it comes to floors, you will unearth a wealth of coverings at second-hand markets. If you discover a beautiful piece, nothing will show it off

ABOVE Thick woollen rugs make hard-wearing chair covers. This old army rug is tacked onto the chair in a big blanket stitch.

ABOVE LEFT Sew squares of handmade antique lace onto plain cushions to give them depth and texture.

LEFT Old Welsh blankets cover a once dishevelled pair of armchairs. Out of the blanket remnants a dog was born.

quite like a white or light wood floor. For patterned looks, search for Turkish kilims or Indian dhurries – or, if you find a carpet you like, simply cut off a piece to use as a rug. Heavy quilts can also work on the floor. Animal skins feel sensuously soft underfoot, so hunt down sheepskin, cowhide, goatskin, fake zebra prints and similar pieces.

Many fabrics found at markets are exceptionally good quality, such as antique linen, classic cotton, thick woollen blankets and handmade lace. Textiles that survive years of servitude do so because they are resilient, and most of these are made of natural fibres. Some pieces may be slightly threadbare, frayed or bleached out, but these timeworn old dames inject a relaxed, lived-in feel to your home.

RIGHT Antique handmade tablecloths make delicate window covers, allowing light to penetrate through the weave while banishing inquisitive eyes.

BELOW Dress up a chair with cushions made out of little black dresses. Former sequinned gowns give this black-linen-covered chair instant glamour.

Like the most durable fabrics, certain prints stand the test of time, including polka dots, stripes (particularly red-white or blue-white stripes), florals, graphic patterns, gingham, animal prints, crochet squares and paisleys. Patterns from different eras work well together (an Art Deco print and a 1950s print, a 1970s paisley print with a 1930s floral design) and look equally alluring with modern prints. As with paint, you can either mix similar patterns or bring together polka dots, stripes and graphics for a bold, audacious look. Remember to make the most of pattern with plain. Your eye will

Heavy quilts and animal hides, such as sheepskin, goatskin and cowhide, make wonderfully soft and sensuous floor coverings.

appreciate a jewel-like collection of cushions on a fresh, white sofa or a patchwork quilt crowned with white linen pillows.

When looking for second-hand fabrics, start with conventional sources, but don't forget that vintage clothing is also a treasure trove of textiles waiting to be resuscitated. Vintage dresses, particularly those with full skirts, have lots of fabric to recycle. To create felt, buy a heap of old woollen jumpers and put them through a hot wash. You can easily fashion these into cushion covers or use them to create a winter-weight patchwork quilt.

Other pieces to look out for are pashminas and ponchos, which – in the same way that you would casually throw one over your naked shoulders – you

RIGHT To achieve a country feel, combine various types of traditional pattern, such as paisleys, florals, checks and stripes.

THIS PAGE You might not think that a polka-dot handkerchief, a geometric scarf, a crocheted rug and two floral cushions would go together, but this artful ensemble is a fine example of effective combining.

OPPOSITE Create your own patchwork quilt from old baby's clothes, vintage dresses, scarves, curtains – whatever you can find. Add a colourful valance made from a disused tablecloth or fabric roll secured by the weight of the mattress.

LEFT Hide pockmarked tables under unusual tablecloths such as this one, created from the end of a fabric bolt. Antique linen sheets and Indian cotton bedspreads make good washable covers.

RIGHT Vintage tea towels made from robust old linens often surface at markets. Choose ones with funky retro designs.

can drape over sofas and armchairs or sew into cushion covers. Other clothes include silk scarves, which can also be used to make beguiling cushion covers or to adorn plain bedside tables. A black lacy shawl could become a window cover (the light will diffuse through it beautifully). If you have no time for sewing, pay a visit to your local tailor and commission a piece. Cushion covers, for example, are a simple job and shouldn't cost much.

More conventional fabric finds, such as curtains, bedspreads and tablecloths, will easily find a use in your home. For example, if you possess a large sofa with a drab cover, a vintage bedspread or curtains swathed over the entire piece will hide a multitude of imperfections. Bedspreads, especially old Indian cotton ones, make funky tablecoths and generously large picnic blankets.

Curtains – such as the plush red velvet variety of curtain popular in the 1980s – can also be adapted to make covers for beds or cushions. Designed as an insulating material, luxurious velvet makes a pragmatic winter bedcover. A patchwork quilt could become a striking living-room wall-hanging or a makeshift curtain in a child's room. Every fabric, conventional or otherwise, has endless possibilities.

One of the most rewarding fabrics to keep your eyes open for is antique linen. Once a treasured heirloom, old linen often turns up in markets. It is unbeatable for softness and resilience – consider, for example, freshly ironed linen sheets scented with lavender. If you find an old linen sheet, but parts of it are threadbare, simply cut it up into tea towels. Do as frugal housewives once did and cut down sheets to make handkerchiefs and window-cleaning rags. Old linen tablecloths once came fringed with hand-stitched lace. When hung on a window, these become

Swathe a vintage bedspread or pair of old curtains over a drab sofa to conceal a multitude of imperfections. Bedspreads can also serve as funky tablecloths.

LEFT Introducing fabrics into an interior space has an immediate softening effect, as demonstrated in this room by a brightly coloured blanket casually thrown over the arm of a sofa. Ethnic rugs of this type were indispensable features of 1960s style – as were flamboyant swirly patterns such as the one seen in the curtain fabric.

perfect blinds, letting in just enough light while simultaneously maintaining privacy. In addition to their obvious uses as soft furnishings, many fabrics can take on more off-beat roles. For an instant artwork, stretch a particularly beautiful piece over an old canvas – or, if you find a dress to die for, model it on a dressmaker's dummy for an instant sculpture.

ABOVE Crochet throws lend a soft, homely feel to several rooms in the home. Sofas, armchairs, daybeds and beds all love curling up with a crochet rug.

THIS PAGE From the
tarnished silver cup to the
antique scent bottle and
the envelope fashioned
out of an old music score,
these pieces come from a
similar palette and share
an otherworldly feel – so
they work well as a group.

RIGHT Soda siphons in green or clear glass are a common sight at markets.

BELOW Create your own sparkling floral display out of crystal chandelier drops and artificial flowers made from antique fabric scraps stretched around pliable piping. Arrange with care in a sturdy vase to match.

Ceramics and glass are the jewels of your interior space. Just as one big ruby pendant can transform a little black dress, so can a single red vase add vibrancy and a touch of drama to a slate-coloured room.

ceramics and glass

Use ceramics and glass to add glamour and beauty to your home. Imagine, for example, a windowsill adorned with a string of sparkling perfume bottles or a table dressed with a necklace of Moroccan tea glasses with glowing tea lights inside.

Allow yourself to be seduced by stall after stall of shapely bowls, elegant vases and candelabra, handsome earthenware pots, dainty glasses and pretty plates. There is a multitude of castaways just begging to be rescued and brought home.

Such beautiful vintage finds are very much in vogue. Open any recent interiors magazine and you'll see how desirable previously loved glassware and ceramics have become. Pieces such as delicate, hand-painted teacups, crystal cake stands and futuristic 1950s vases are selling like hot cakes

ABOVE Ceramic and glass
vessels make colourful,
elegant containers for
everyday kitchen herbs.

RIGHT Unusual flowers
bring a born-again quality
to second-hand vases.

OPPOSITE, MAIN
PICTURE This set of
large, sculptural vases had
a rather macabre past life
as containers for graveyard
flowers. Now packed with
hydrangeas and reborn in a
dining-room table display,
they are full of life's joys.

OPPOSITE, INSET A
Grecian urn-shaped vase is
given a contemporary spin
with a bouquet of sunny
yellow roses.

Allow yourself to be seduced by stall after stall of shapely bowls, vases and candelabra, handsome earthenware pots, dainty glasses and pretty plates.

at markets and seem to be usurping their modern counterparts in many homes. This may be because vintage items introduce a bit of soul into clean-lined modern interiors – or because they retain an artistry that is lost in mass-produced pieces.

With decades of different styles to choose from you will find pieces to satisfy your own taste. Go retro with chunky, funky 1950s pots, or go classical with large Roman pots. People with a penchant for global style can mix traditional English pale blue-and-white Wedgwood plates (which can also be valuable) with aqua-blue glazed tagines from the

Middle East. Country-style lovers will revel in the assortment of floral vases or stripy ceramics. If minimalism is your thing, rummage for Japanese-style tea sets and celadon rice bowls to adorn otherwise naked windowsills.

While many ceramic and glass vessels have their conventional uses, you can create unusual features with everyday items. Chinese vases, for example, double as beautiful storage pots, while long-necked vases work as candelabra, and dainty milk jugs make elegant desk tidies. Old jam jars serve as beautiful lanterns for candles, as do other vessels,

OPPOSITE Display your glass jewels in a place where they can be properly admired. This collection of seconds and samples from a glassware factory adorn simple glass shelves. They have been placed in such a way as to catch the sun, so that a rainbow of light falls around a Plain Jane room.

particularly multi-coloured glass dessert bowls or blue-glass wine goblets. Extra large pieces, such as old Chinese vases or Arabic earthenware pots, can be transformed into umbrella stands.

Many ceramic or glass finds make original flower vases. Second-hand finds let you create startling, eye-catching looks with unusual pairings. Put big blooms in dainty teacups, for example, or gather a few gerbera in an old wine decanter. You could adorn eggcups with individual carnation heads or put pink roses in Moroccan tea glasses.

Old milk jugs, kitchen jars, tea caddies, large mugs and teapots make unusual containers in which to grow parsley, sage, dill, basil and other culinary herbs on a sunny windowsill. Grow a fern in a ceramic chamber pot, or crown a low-level vase with long grasses. For plants that need constant water, drill holes in the bottom of containers using a drill bit appropriate for the material. Put these planters on old saucers or big plain dinner plates.

Ceramic tiles are junk must-haves. When new owners move into a house, they often strip out old pieces in the cause of modernization, and beautiful orphans can always be found at second-hand shops. These hand-made pieces possess a warmth and workmanship that distinguishes them from their mass-produced counterparts. Look out for old white and blue Delftware tiles, graphic 1970s-style tiles and traditional terracotta tiles. Being heat-resistant, these pieces can become useful coasters or hotplates. If you can find enough tiles of the same style (or mix your finds with new pieces), use them to make kitchen splashbacks or to add visual interest to bathroom tiles.

When buying your pieces, keep in mind where they will live. Remember that one beautiful piece is often more eye-catching than a cluster of items.

LEFT So kitsch – and yet so beautiful. A Japanese-style ceramic sculpture of a blossoming tree has been turned into a convenient jewellery stand, used to store – and to show off – the owner's collection of theatrical earrings.

Cherish your collections. A wall of plates, a shelf of teapots or a window ledge of French milk jugs can make a beautiful focal point.

ABOVE Invent new uses for old vessels. No longer needed as goblets, these gilt-edged Danish twins are now glamorous vases.

LEFT Cracked and chipped but by no means down and out, a pair of perfume bottles are born again as ornaments. To attract attention to their comely figures, they have been adorned with jewels and artificial butterflies.

ABOVE RIGHT Many glass tumblers, goblets, bowls and dishes can be reused as candle-holders, as exemplified by this petite, pretty glass beaker.

You will need to give your special piece enough space to breathe – place it in an alcove or against a white wall, for example; if it has star qualities, put it on show by shining a traditional brass picture light on it, or frame it with fairy lights.

If you want to group things on window ledges and shelves, buy pieces that vary in height and size and use the 'family photo' principle, with large pieces at the back and small ones at the front. Mix rough with smooth, contrasting dark against light and playing shiny pieces off matt pieces. Groups of items often grow organically. Once you have acquired a taste for an era, style or type of object, you may find yourself inadvertently creating a collection of vases, teacups, eggcups or glasses.

THIS PAGE From the ceramic serving plates to the silver coffee pot, this beautiful collection of kitchenware should prompt you to hurry down to your local market and scour the stalls for classic items.

Gud velsigne vort Hjem

RIGHT It is unusual to find a set of matching plates at a market. Instead, you can assemble a dining set from an eclectic mixture of handsome plates.

RIGHT It is unusual to find a set of matching plates at a market. Instead, you can assemble a dining set from an eclectic mixture of handsome plates.

Items such as oversized copper pots, dainty crystal cake stands, tiny gold salt bowls with fine spoons and solid–silver cutlery were once so cherished that pieces were passed down through the generations – and now they are turning up at markets.

kitchenware

BELOW You can store rice, flour, sugar, pasta, biscuits and other groceries in vintage containers such as this assortment of kitsch, colourful retro tins.

Once upon a time, in an era before TV dinners, cooking, serving and savouring food was a serious affair. The average time spent preparing evening meals in Britain was 60 minutes, while today it is a mere 13 minutes. Yet the rise of the TV dinner has proved a blessing for flea-market aficionados (and food lovers), who can now furnish their kitchens with beautiful, built-to-last cookware.

Many kitchen items have survived because they are robust, fashioned by artisans from good-quality materials. And there is something special about the warmth of a hand-painted bone-china cup that leaves a mass-produced mug in the shade. The errant line of a hand-beaten silver spoon has a more human quality than the over-smooth look of a piece straight off the factory production line.

Second-hand tableware will provide endless topics for dinner-party conversation. The discovery of each piece is often a story in itself. What's more, your finds may inspire culinary experimentation. If you like dinner parties with a twist, dine in with 1970s-style fondue sets and heart-shaped jelly moulds.

Continuing the second-hand theme, serve food on an array of mismatching dinner plates. If you can't find a matching dinner set, create your own from pieces chosen according to colour or pattern (all blue-themed plates, for example). You will also find a wealth of cutlery at markets. Again, pick pieces of a similar style, delving deep for once-sought-after bone-handled utensils, which are lovely to hold (but not dishwasher-friendly) and three-pronged silver Georgian forks.

Serve your guests drinks from your found array of old tumblers, pint glasses and – for serious beer drinkers – Toby jugs. Scour markets for wine glasses with a similar look or shape, such as thin-stemmed red wine glasses with large bowls.

Champagne bowls reminiscent of *Breakfast at Tiffany's* sometimes put their pretty heads above the parapet at markets. These graceful glasses went out of fashion because the flute shape was found to keep champagne's bubbles for longer – but, if you believe that there is no reason not to quaff champagne quickly, invest in a set of mismatching bowls. Hunt down other drinks accessories such

OPPOSITE Once you start collecting orphaned pieces, you could soon find yourself with cupboards bursting with finds. This owner has collected items according to their culinary use – for example, oriental-style rice bowls and 1950s, pastel-coloured tea cups. Other collections include espresso cups, casserole dishes, salad bowls, milk jugs and dining plates.

as sherry decanters, ice buckets, ice tongs, wine coolers, waiter's corkscrews and bottle openers.

One reason why antique glasses and ceramics have come back into fashion is the return of social occasions based on food rituals, such as coffee mornings and afternoon tea parties. Coffee lovers will find plenty of retro coffee pots and percolators as well as examples of wooden coffee grinders and branded coffee-bean jars. Graphically decorated cups and saucers are always good retro buys.

Second-hand markets also serve up an array of tea paraphernalia – themed teapots, tea cosies, milk jugs, delicate sugar bowls, sugar-cube tongs,

ABOVE These eclectic finds have all been cherry-picked over years from the same big flea market in Brussels. The discerning owner has treasured pieces for their individual beauty, collecting shapes, colours and sizes from a range of different eras. Where possible, he has bought matching sets or hunted down groups of pieces with similar themes.

Antique glasses and ceramics have come back into vogue with the return of coffee mornings, tea parties and other events based on food rituals.

OPPOSITE AND LEFT
Many divorced teacups turn up as singles at markets. Re-marry them to saucer finds, pairing gilt-edged floral cups with gilt-edged floral saucers, for example. Alternatively, use single teacups as tiny vases for single blooms or bouquets of wildflowers, or dot tea lights inside and use them as candle-holders.

RIGHT, ABOVE AND BELOW People who love baking will simply feast on market offerings. From old-style measuring spoons to themed-shaped cake tins and cookie cutters, there is a wealth of once-loved culinary items. Look for old wooden spoons, flour sifters, hand eggbeaters and big ceramic bowls.

and strainers – but what they do best is teacups. Your chance of finding a complete set is very slim, so look for pieces that harmonize, such as an assortment of gold-rimmed china cups or dainty floral designs. To serve accompanying cakes, snap up a 1950s crystal cake stand or a tiered stand in silver and pair it with an ornate silver cake knife.

When it comes to cookware, you will find plenty of examples of large wooden spoons, kettles, old copper pots, soup ladles, cookie cutters, ice-cream scoops, rolling pins, nutcrackers, old-fashioned egg beaters and, with luck, old scales complete with measuring weights – as well as other kitchen paraphernalia (floral tin flour sifters with handles, measuring spoons, pressure cookers, glass juicers).

When you have acquired such beautiful old things, you definitely don't want to hide them in your drawers, so display lovely serving dishes on racks or hang your old-style copper pots and pans from a rack with butchers' hooks.

Lighting seems like a detail – yet nothing can transform a room as radically. Turn a spotlight on an elegant vase or light a single naked flame in a dark room – and notice how the whole room is born again.

lighting

OPPOSITE Although this space is open plan, the two oriental-style, ball-shaped pendant lights define the dining space. The 'masterpiece' behind the table is an old piece of patterned linoleum hung from bulldog clips on nails.

RIGHT Ornate glass-drop wall sconces, with a duet of golden pleated shades, create a glamorous focal point by day, and, with the engraved mirror behind, provide a warm wash of light by night.

Let's start with the practicalities. When you are out shopping, there are three kinds of household lights to look out for: general lighting (for long dark nights), task lighting (for performing particular, close-up tasks) and feature lighting (for aesthetics).

The only caveat to bear in mind when buying second-hand light fittings is to examine them for any signs of wear and tear such as exposed or loose wiring or bent socket pegs. If you have any doubts, get your lights checked and installed by a qualified electrician who can replace and rewire worn or damaged fittings.

For general lighting, keep your eyes open for a range of lights but take into account the shape, size and function of the room in question. Living rooms are for relaxation and conversation, so the lighting in them needs to be soft and convivial, never brash, bright or hospital-like. If your living room is pint-sized, create optical illusions with lights – for example, wall sconces provide a wash of light across the walls, making them appear larger. Eschew long-hanging or large bold pendant lights in small rooms because these tend to draw the eye downwards, making ceilings seem lower.

General lighting should illuminate an entire room at the flick of a switch. It can take the form of wall sconces, standard lamps or pendant fittings, with or without shades. Wall sconces from all eras turn up at second-hand stalls since these are often orphaned when people tear out old fittings to create clean lines in new homes. There is always a good selection of second-hand lamps at markets, some discarded from former factories or made redundant from offices. These pieces may require some tender loving customization, such as the repainting of a shade or the replacement of a base. If you discover a pendant shade that is the right size but not the right appearance, fashion your own cover from vintage fabric finds (think old curtains, second-hand skirts or shawls), or customize it with ribbons, buttons, beads or fake flowers.

One timeless second-hand find is a chandelier. Some come with cherubs and others have kitsch fake candles with flame-shaped bulbs, but the ones

ABOVE Avoid eye strain when reading in bed. Simply re-purpose an office desk light or a floor-standing lamp, which can be easily adjusted to direct light onto the book at hand.

RIGHT For an innovative reading lamp, use a clamp-on desk light on a chair's backrest, as shown here.

OPPOSITE An industrial-style floor-standing lamp suits the restrained style of this work space. While the owner could have repainted the light, its chipped and careworn looks complement the distressed paintwork of the rickety chair.

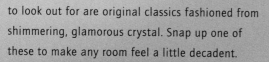

LEFT Elegant glass drops dangling from metal fronds have been added to an industrial light to form a 'chandelier'. Alternative, similar drops might include colourful beads, ribbons or flower garlands.

BELOW This metal floral bouquet, of a type that came and went in a flicker during the 1950s, is a style of fitting that you are likely to see on your expeditions.

RIGHT If your horizons are global, seek out light shades such as this one, from a Moroccan market.

to look out for are original classics fashioned from shimmering, glamorous crystal. Snap up one of these to make any room feel a little decadent.

When it comes to task lighting, simply search for the right light for the job. For home offices, look out for anglepoise lamps, but ensure that the springs are operational. If they are too loose, you will end up with a floppy light; if they are too tight, you won't be able to adjust them. In living rooms, you will need reading sidelights (or angled wall sconces) and in bedrooms, bedside reading lights. Think laterally. An old desk lamp could easily make a bedside table light. Table lamps are

easy to create yourself. Introduce single items to each other to make beautiful marriages, such as an antique iron base and a funky 1950s shade, or a solid wooden base and a pleated pastel shade.

Feature lighting highlights a little of what you fancy. Use it to accent your most-loved possessions (use a downlighter, for example, to draw attention to a loved painting). Alternatively, you can choose old lights as pieces to adore for their own beauty. If you love a chandelier's sense of grandeur but don't want to wire it up, simply hang it near a window so it reflects the daylight. Other antique lights simply look handsome, such as ornate gas

THIS PICTURE Just as diamonds are a girl's best friend, so chandeliers are a room's best friend. If it is too complicated to adapt your chandelier find to light a modern room, use it as decoration and hang it where the natural light can catch its sparkly drops.

lights from yesteryear. For an air of otherworldly romance, look for strings of fairy lights. Some may require new bulbs or have missing decorations, so customize them with other finds, such as fake flowers or butterflies. If you want to accent pieces of artwork, search out traditional brass picture lights or frame a painting with fairy lights.

Most of your creativity will go into lighting your principal rooms, but keep the junk feeling alive in hallways and entrances and on staircases. It is easy to disregard these spaces, but funky lights help to make the most of what might otherwise be forgotten passageways. Dot mismatching second-hand lamps up the staircase, for example, or run a length of fairy lights down a hallway to create eye-catching features. Of course, first impressions

RIGHT Pair lighting finds like this lovely blue base with a vintage lampshade. If a base is in good shape but the shade is past help, re-cover the shade's frame with a vintage fabric or wallpaper find.

OPPOSITE Fairy lights can create alluring shapes on walls. If a set of fairy lights have lost their decorations, you could fashion your own light garland from artificial butterflies or flowers.

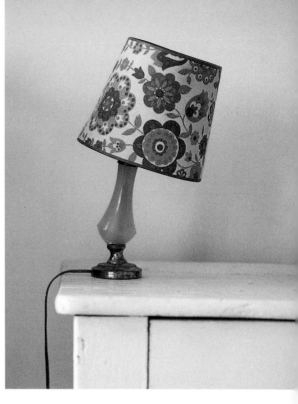

Create a magical, mystical atmosphere at night by dotting lit candles around the house – in clusters in corners of the bathroom, in lines across the mantelpiece – and lighting a solitary flame in the bedroom.

LEFT A cherub balances on her hand a quartet of long, thin candles, adding old-world glamour to a clean-lined modern kitchen.

count, so ensure that your entranceway is well lit. This is the place to position one spectacular find, such as a customized chandelier or a big bold floor lamp with a graphic lampshade.

In conclusion, remember that the style of light that never dates is candlelight. There is nothing more evocative than a naked flame. While you may not find many wax candles at second-hand markets, you will find a glittery array of beautiful things to put them in – including old storm lanterns, oil lamplighters and grand silver heirloom candelabra. Many unconventional discoveries, such as vintage bottles, old vases, coloured tumblers and crystal dessert bowls, also make beautiful candle-holders.

OPPOSITE Collections are about whatever you want them to be. This mix of fossils, florets of coral, silver cups, candle-holders, trinkets and stuffed animals is the height of eclecticism.

RIGHT Tickle your fancy with fistfuls of coloured feathers in glass jars.

If there are certain items that you are passionate about, you may find yourself buying one more . . . and another. Gradually the hunt reaches fever-pitch and, before you know it, you have acquired a collection.

collections and display

ABOVE Exhibit your loved things for all to see (but not for little fingers to touch) in glass-fronted cabinets.

RIGHT A beautiful effigy of the Virgin Mary models a selection of necklaces, while a group of pictures and portraits behind the statue preserves memories.

Creating a collection is about bringing together beautiful things that you adore and indulging your whims. Whether you are in love with oil paintings, peacock feathers, army buttons, vintage clothes, 1930s vases, antique jewellery, fake flowers, pop memorabilia, tin soldiers or leather-bound poetry books, your hunt will take on a life of its own. Collecting brings out the hoarder in all of us.

Art collectors, for example, love markets, where whole galleries of pictures await them. Choose pieces by genre – old oil paintings, for example – or by theme, such as landscapes, flower displays, portraits or dogs. Instead of just hanging pieces in conventional places, you could display them by grouping them on a wall or placing them on the floor along the length of a corridor. If you assemble a collection of pictures whose frames don't look right together, simply remove the frames and hang works from bulldog clips nailed to the wall or from pegs clipped to an old washing

ABOVE AND ABOVE LEFT Markets are full of old oil paintings, but artists' palettes are rarer. Display your artistic gems against a canvas of white.

LEFT Hang pictures in groups for impact, but allow a bit of breathing space between them.

RIGHT Instead of using conventional frames, hang your photographs from the wall by bulldog clips attached to nails.

LEFT When you follow your instincts and make impulse buys at different markets, you will often end up, over time, with various examples on the same theme, such as this pack of dog portraits.

line. Otherwise, you could repaint the frames or replace them with beautiful alternatives, such as driftwood frames.

If you prefer photographic images, possible finds range from sepia-coloured portraits to black and white landscapes. If your own ancestor collection does not amount to much, adopt other people's photographs by buying old family photograph albums from markets. Postcards can also be worth treasuring. To display such memorabilia, string them up with paperclips or safety pins, or tack them onto walls to make a collage.

If you can't find any pieces of art or sculptures you like, devise your own masterpiece. Take, for example, one empty gilt frame and hang it on a blank wall. Within its gilt-edged boundary, simply tack up pieces you love, such as pinned butterflies or fake corsages sprayed with glitter dust – or create still-lives from personal mementoes such as perfume bottles, once-loved toys, dried roses or coins acquired on foreign travels.

Mirrors, like paintings, look glamorous when grouped together, creating a feeling of light and space. Even a series of hand mirrors hung from a

ABOVE Other finds for walls might include old maps, like the one shown here, pieces of vintage wallpaper, antique fabrics stretched over canvases and linoleum offcuts.

wall look stunning. Choose pieces with different shapes or similar frames and use them to bring light into a dark corner like a stairwell or hallway.

Many fashionistas dedicate their flea-market legwork to finding beautiful vintage clothes as well as handbags, hats, shoes and boots. Instead of letting these pieces languish like wallflowers in wardrobes, put them on display. For example, you

Many natural items turn up at markets – pieces of driftwood, coral, starfish, fossils or semi–precious stones such as amethysts.

could clothe a dressmaker's model in your favourite dress or simply hang much-loved pieces from coat hangers in open wardrobes or against wardrobe doors. Display shoes from a series of mini shelves or frame them in alcoves as if in a shop. Handbags and hats look dramatic when hung in groups from nails on the wall.

Other fashion accessories, such as feathers, fake corsages, brooches, ribbons, hairclips, lace and dress pins, can be used to transform cushions, rugs, and other home accessories. If you find some old brooches, for example, simply pin them onto one of your vintage cushions. Customize an old lampshade by tying a beautiful ribbon around it, or stick a series of feathers in its cap to give it instant panache. For a festive mood, create show-stopping

OPPOSITE, FAR LEFT AND CENTRE Use found objects to fashion your own still life on a sideboard. Here, some old coffee tins have been given a decorative makeover.

OPPOSITE, RIGHT Display your vintage clothing collection on a dressmaker's model and change her dress weekly.

THIS PAGE Think about how to organize and show off your finds to best visual advantage. For example, pieces of found wood could be arranged in groups like long, thin ethnic figurines, as shown here, or made to stand to attention along a shelf (see inset).

LEFT AND RIGHT Instead of hiding your beautiful clothes, bags and shoes behind cupboard doors, put them where they can strut their stuff. Display them along a wall on coat-hangers hung from nails or picture hooks – or hang them from a metal kitchen rack. Recycle classic jackets and coats and keep your eyes peeled for good-quality, sturdy, wooden coathangers.

BELOW Use capacious market bags as storage for your socks, lingerie and handkerchiefs.

RIGHT Store beautiful little things – feathers, buttons, ribbons, thread, theatrical jewellery, string, buttons, safety pins – in glass jars and use them to customize your outfits or your home's interior. In this room, domestic pipes support an impromptu display of fake flowers, letters and toys. From the pipes hang butchers' hooks festooned with Christmas baubles and necklaces.

garlands with a collection of artificial corsages strung together on a piece of coloured string or a long length of ribbon. You could also hang and clip ribbons, artificial flowers and butterflies and bead necklaces to wire coat hangers (weave a couple together by the handles) to create a mobile for a children's bedroom. If you have found a chandelier with missing drops, such *objets trouvés* make gorgeous replacements.

Jewellery collections should never languish in a trinket box. Add glamour to walls, paintings, chairs and bedheads with strings of pearls, diamonds, opal pendants and shimmering silver chains. If you have some glittery glass beads, string them up on windows and mirrors or over lampshades so that they reflect the light, sending little coloured rays around the room.

Many natural items turn up at markets – pieces of driftwood, coral, starfish, fossils or semi-precious stones such as amethysts. Put such natural wonders

LEFT AND BELOW A collection of rosaries and crosses, some hanging from an ornate carved bedhead, adds an air of spirituality to a bedroom.

FAR LEFT From old postcards and photographs to mirrors and necklaces, the collection of intimate images on this wall makes an original display.

where they can be appreciated or use them to create original works of art. Fashion driftwood into a photograph or mirror frame or drill tiny holes in a smooth, organic-shaped piece to put your sticks of incense in.

Most market aficionados are inevitably drawn towards the second-hand book and magazine section since there will always be something there to covet. From dusty copies of Charles Dickens's *Oliver Twist* to ancient Mickey Mouse comics, you are likely to discover something to stimulate your imagination on virtually every subject.

If you collect old magazines, you can always tear out pages and use them to make picture collages

RIGHT AND OPPOSITE Walls make wonderful canvases for the display of market-found objects such as beads, shell necklaces, old postcards and hand-stitched lace. Other finds, such as dried flowers and autumn leaves, come from nature itself. Beautiful, fragile pieces like these allow you to create a 'found' artwork against a plain backdrop.

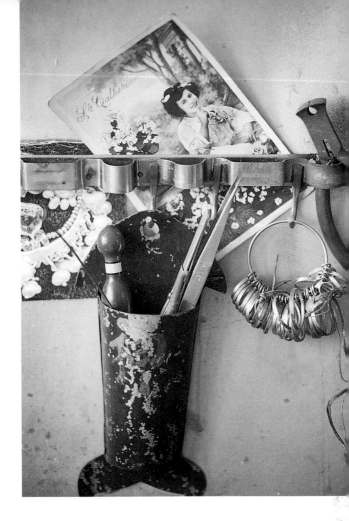

to adorn your walls. Or, to enliven children's rooms, you could paste up pages from old comics to create original wallpaper that will absorb the little ones for hours. When it comes to displaying your literary finds, the conventional choices are bookshelves and office shelving, but for an alternative display you could stack your books spines outward in colour-coded towers up and down a hallway.

Try to maintain the spirit of a collection in the way you display it. If you have gathered together fragile pieces – such as old perfume bottles, china figurines or dainty teacups, for example – keep them protected from inquisitive small fingers by storing them in Art Deco cabinets with lockable glass doors. If you have decided to hoard early editions of classic books, think about storing them in a complementary weathered-wood bookshelf from a similar period – or contrast their fine old looks by showing them off in a plastic modern modular shelving system.

Instead of hiding your beautiful serving dishes at the back of your kitchen cupboards, display them as they would have been in former times on wooden racks, hung from the wall or on country-style sideboards with display shelves. Look for a Victorian tea trolley on which to show off your dainty teacups, saucers and teapots.

While many collections call for conventional display, think about how to arrange your treasured pieces in unusual places for maximum impact. Our eyes – like our ears – often fail to appreciate items that are presented to us in clichéd ways, so think about offbeat alternatives. If you have fallen for 1950s vases, for example, line the whole lot up like soldiers along the centre of a table and crown them with big blooms. Or present your collection of old bottles by ranging them along a window ledge

(the light will highlight the glass), and fill your disused fireplace with vintage vases. Eye-catching pieces demand eye-catching displays.

If you collect odd bits and bobs, you will need to store them – and you could create a subsidiary collection from the boxes you put them in. You might, for example, buy a series of small leather suitcases in which to store a collection of costume jewellery or old coins – or you could use a roll of vintage wallpaper to cover cardboard boxes of all shapes and sizes. Old gym lockers, which provide generous storage, sometimes surface at markets, while mail-sorting shelves or stacked wine boxes could be transformed into open pigeonholes that will allow you to savour your much-loved finds.

ABOVE A ring collection is displayed on a sculptural hand. The owner has also collected Indian tin boxes, which she has ingeniously turned into wall shelving.

RIGHT A jewellery-maker has collected vintage photographs to provide her with inspiration.

OPPOSITE, LEFT AND ABOVE RIGHT Letters from shop fronts and printing blocks can make interesting collections. Look for your own initials.

OPPOSITE, BELOW RIGHT Even storage like these towering stacks of boxes could form the basis of a collection.

putting it all together

Flea-market style is by its nature relaxing and comforting to live with because junk pieces with past lives are never precious, uptight or pretentious; they have been there, done that – and lived to tell the tale.

relaxing spaces

LEFT Plenty of fabrics, from the floral cushion covers to the large skin on the floor, soften the feel of this industrial-style London warehouse. From the Guy Rogers daybed to the nut-brown Chesterfield sofa, all these pieces have been chosen for their classic looks. Ethnic finds, such as the Moroccan pouf and the little African table, add a note of eclectic chic.

When trying to create a relaxing space in flea-market style, the big backdrops – floors and walls – really count. If you want to include patterned furniture, make your backdrops plain; paint or paper walls in a neutral colour and keep floors monochrome. If your living area is small, use optical illusion: light walls and floors will make the space look bigger, while dark canvases make the space look smaller. Mirrors double the light in a room, so harness their powers. Choose one large mirror (such as a former dressing-table mirror or full-length dressmaker's mirror) or create a mixture of styles by hanging a variety of mirrors on one wall.

If you like pattern but don't want to sacrifice a sense of space, decorate a single wall in vintage wallpaper, putting plain furniture in front of it. Strips of wallpaper or textured wallpapers also create funky backdrops. Consider stripped, stained or painted wooden floors. Soften the look, and reduce noise, with textile finds such as old animal skins, including cowhides, goatskins and sheepskins, and rugs, such as Indian dhurries, Persian prayer mats and woven hearth rugs. Old carpets, which are frequently the first thing new owners strip out, also create foot-friendly floor covers. Simply cut them to the size you require. Your

Signs of having been loved – a coffee–cup blemish on a table, a worn patch on an armrest, a slight indent on a sofa – make flea–market finds easy to accommodate.

living room is one of the main public areas in the home, so it is worth taking time to style it to your satisfaction. Most living rooms are organized around a single focal point such as a hearth, the home's traditional heartland. Seating is often grouped around a low-level table (think kidney tables, tables made from old railway sleepers, retro chrome and glass tables). Arrange your furniture in groups for conviviality, with sofas facing each other

ABOVE **If you are lucky, you may stumble across design classics such as this red Ercol sofa, adorned with a jewel-like collection of cushions. An ethnic rug provides warmth and softness underfoot.**

or armchairs set in a circle. If you don't like sitting shoulder to shoulder with others on a sofa, then assemble a collection of slouchy armchairs; it won't matter that they don't match since they'll all share a laid-back look.

If your fireplace is meant to be a focal point, give it eye-catching style. Markets are home to old accessories, including wrought-iron fireguards, coal scuttles, copper bellows, cinder brushes and pokers. The advent of the contemporary 'hole-in-the-wall' fireplace has been responsible for many new homeowners stripping out beautiful old fireplaces and mantelpieces. Restore the glamour of an old fireplace, but before lighting up have the chimney inspected and cleaned by a professional, and bone up on the fuel-burning regulations in your area. Many urban areas require secondary burners for coal or wood fires to keep down pollution levels.

Lighting is the next priority. Living rooms need a combination of lights for different purposes. Apart from the vast choice of pendant lights on offer at markets, softer options include former office-desk lights for sofa-side reading and Victorian wall sconces for shining a wash of light on a wall, which has the bonus of making the room feel lighter and bigger. Everyone glows under the gentle light of a naked flame, so seek out discarded storm lanterns or candleholders of all sorts.

The most important buys for your relaxing room are the pieces of furniture. Finding a sofa that fits you and your style has the same effect as buying a comfortable bed. When you get home, you'll never want to move. It is worth emphasizing that you should always try out furniture before making a purchase. A sofa, for example, may be good to look at, but if you sit on it you may find that its springs are shot or its frame is broken. If you like lying on

THIS PAGE Juxtapose pieces with a similar feel. In this living room, timeless classics, from the black leather Chesterfield sofa (whose ripped arm is covered by a throw) to the ornate side table, combine to create a refined, elegant look. In the absence of a sideboard, the drinks have been stashed in a large wooden wardrobe.

THIS PAGE This sleek contemporary room is given a lived-in feel with found furniture. A chest of drawers, repainted white, provides storage, while a former desk offers a display surface for 1970s-style graphic vases.

THIS PAGE This living room, with its to-die-for beige leather sofa, looks eclectic but elegant. Its canvases – the white walls and glossy black floor – make the perfect backdrop for a sculptural lamp, a cushion fashioned from a silk scarf and a portrait of the young Queen.

OPPOSITE **Create a haven for relaxation in an unexpected corner. In this guest bedroom, a chair upholstered in a soft, worn velvet cover makes an ideal place for repose. Peg rails, normally used in hallways, give extra hanging space for visitors' coats and bags.**

ABOVE **Set against a backdrop of neutral floor and walls, this chintzy old sofa looks as good today as it did over 30 years ago.**

sofas, make sure that whichever one you plan to purchase is the right size. And, don't judge a sofa by its cover. You can always use vintage fabric finds or dyed sheets, ex-army rugs and old curtains to re-upholster or re-cover an aged sofa. The repair process is not quite as simple in the case of leather sofas, since getting a leather sofa re-upholstered can be as expensive as buying a new one. If black leather is ripped or worn, you could patch it up with tape; if the arm of your brown leather sofa has started to look worn, wrap it in a cover. Many of us have already adopted and developed styles for our interior spaces based on trends of the moment. One popular contemporary look combines old world glamour with a minimalist twist, for example. Paint your floorboards and walls white, then choose a couple of beautiful pieces, such as a large nut-brown leather sofa, an elaborate mirror or one eye-catching pendant light, and soften the look with cushions made from luxurious second-hand fabric discoveries, including pashmina shawls, cashmere jerseys or silk dressing gowns.

BELOW A self-confessed lover of flea-markets, the owner of this apartment has based his seating arrangement on two good-quality sofas fashioned out of stiff, resilient calico. To protect their handsome visage, the sofas have been covered in thick blankets.

RIGHT Old leather club chairs sit comfortably side by side, flanking a classic lamp, originally designed for industrial use in the 1950s. Pieces like these are worth paying a little more for, particularly if they are in good condition, since they will retain their value.

Use vintage fabric finds, old curtains or ex-army rugs to revive an old sofa.

Retro lovers will need to flip a few coins to choose between the wonderful range of sofas on offer. Low-level vinyl sofas or coloured leather sofas were once all the rage. When teamed with 1960s wooden sideboards or plastic modular storage, these pieces swing again in their original living-room setting. Complete the look with cushions in graphic prints and vintage 1960s rugs or cuts of 1960s and 1970s carpets. Bean bags in good condition are also inviting.

When it comes to retro lighting, you can often find lights that fit the appropriate colour scheme, such as, for example, plastic orange-shaded mushroom lights and large swooping floor chrome

THIS PAGE This down-to-earth apartment in New York provides a perfect escape from the fast-pace of city life. One of its outstanding features is a pair of birdcages – a rarely spotted market find.

lights (such as Castiglioni's 'Swan' lamp). Markets are often full of chunky 1950s and graphic 1960s vases in which to show off flowers. Hang pot plants from the roof in macramé pot-plant holders.

Devotees of Modernist and Bauhaus pieces will also, if they are fortunate, uncover 20th-century classics with which to enliven their relaxing spaces. Finds of this kind can sometimes be valuable.

ABOVE This classic button-back sofa has been re-upholstered in thick, hard-wearing, former army blankets and accessorized with a Welsh blanket, a found cushion and a pillow covered with jute. Hanging on the wall behind the sofa is a quirky collection of plates and pictures that has gone to the dogs.

THIS PAGE This sofa has received a makeover in the form of a canvas cover. For a deconstructed look, seams are left on the outside. To create a clash of eras, an elaborate old frame borders a modern painting. Two empty picture frames have been given a career change, becoming lightshades.

Originals or close reproductions of classics such as an Eileen Gray 'Bibendum' chair, Arne Jacobson's 'Swan' chair, Verner Panton's plastic 'S' chair or Tom Dixon's 'Jack' light turn up from time to time in markets. If you come across pieces of this kind in good condition, snap them up instantly because their value will only increase with time, while their looks remain timeless. More common pieces found at markets include bent chrome and leather chairs. Soften modernist lines with cow hides on the floor or sew cushions out of zebra prints.

Soften a minimalist look with cushions covered in luxurious second–hand fabric finds, including silk dressing gowns, pashmina shawls or cashmere jerseys.

If you hanker after a country look, flea-market finds will fulfil your rustic desires. Since your most expensive purchase for a relaxing space is likely to be a sofa, buy one that optimizes the look, such as a large, slightly saggy version covered with loose linen chintz, and pile it with crocheted rugs, tartan rugs and throws. If your discovery is the correct shape but needs a new dress, clothe it in striped ticking fabrics or a hardwearing canvas. Chairs to complete the look include old rocking chairs, wicker Lloyd Loom chairs, patio-style wooden chairs and benches made out of rustic woods.

If you need side tables for vases, reading books and table lights, look for school desks and outdoor furniture such as wrought-iron garden tables with mosaic tops. Posies of wild flowers and bouquets of roses in odd found vessels such as bone-china tea cups, rustic French milk jugs and vintage bottles bring life and freshness to your space.

Relaxing spaces are not limited to living rooms. Other places of relaxation at home include nooks and crannies such as the end of a hallway, a space under the stairs or a large stair landing. Wherever it is quiet or where the sunlight falls is potentially a place to park. Flea markets offer up equally odd pieces on which you can recline, including colourful canvas hammocks, homemade swings, roll-out tatami mats and even blow-up Lilos. Since you are a flea-market shopper, you must be used to thinking outside the conventions of a matching three-piece suite, so seek out something original, something that will really help you to relax.

Flea–market style will give a kitchen a cherished and lived–in feel. From big old biscuit tins to solid coffee pots and huge frying pans, formerly loved pieces add to the kitchen's magnetism.

cooking & eating spaces

LEFT AND ABOVE RIGHT There is no need for kitchen pieces bought at flea markets to match. Second-hand finds will allow you to create an original space with timeless furnishings and accessories for next to nothing.

You could, if you wanted to, furnish your cooking and eating spaces with almost everything sourced from flea markets – including the kitchen sink. One good reason for doing so is the sense of tradition that market-found objects bring to these spaces. Most of us continue to cook and eat as we always have done, but time spent preparing meals has steadily diminished. While the generation of home cooks before us spent up to an hour each night preparing the family meal, our increasingly fast-paced lives have reduced this time to mere minutes.

But, however long food takes to cook or prepare, most of us still love the rituals of dining – relishing, for example, the solid feel of thick silver cutlery, the taste of water poured into tumblers from an elegant glass jug and the bouquet of wine served from thin-stemmed, wide-bowled wine glasses. And we are still magnetized by the feel-good warmth of a big kitchen table.

Where cooking and eating rooms were customarily separate, in modern homes they are often rolled into one big space, in which the eating area combines with

RIGHT This extensive collection of crockery, all found at a Brussels market and stacked according to the vessels' uses, colours or eras, is given a home in a huge built-in skyscraper of a shelf, reached by means of an extendable ladder.

ABOVE Mismatched chairs, retouched in pastel shades of eggshell paint, sit attentively at a long, thin table covered by a found yellow linen table runner. Dried hydrangea heads in former graveyard vases add to the faded, otherworldly beauty of this sun-filled eating space.

the food preparation area, farmhouse-style. And, while a kitchen table is used for food preparation and the eating of meals, it is also the place where people gather for long conversations, homework, games or other leisure activities.

When it comes to furnishing your cooking and dining space, the first thing you need to do is decide what kind of look you want to achieve. If you already have a sleek contemporary kitchen, you can add a handful of vintage one-offs to give it a little soul. Contemporary off-the-peg kitchens can

look too high-tech and clinical, but old pieces give them depth and character. And these slick, modern kitchens make clean-lined canvases against which you can show off your fabulous finds.

Modern doesn't have to mean buying new. For a modern classic look in the kitchen, keep the feel minimalist, hiding clutter behind smooth cupboard doors. Display finds such as one curvaceous 1960s vase with flowers on a mantelpiece and, if you do show your kitchenwares, ensure that they are space-enhancing (a shiny silver milk jug or a chrome

toaster, for example), classic (a silver hob kettle or a Romanesque water jug) or elegant (second-hand champagne flutes or a tall retro coffee pot).

Add depth to a contemporary eating space by adorning your swanky, shop-bought, glass-top table with one beautiful antique candelabrum. There's no need to buy new chairs when second-hand markets are overflowing with an array of modern classics such as bent chrome and leather chairs, bentwood café chairs and moulded-plastic 1960s chairs. You can always fashion your own dinner table from a smooth, repainted door mounted on trestles or an old boardroom table.

If you want to clad a modern table in a classic gown, look out for white linen and damask napery (matching tablecloth and napkins). Once given as wedding presents or passed down as heirlooms, these beautiful sets make rare appearances at markets. If you can't find a set, an ensemble of non-matching napery is easy to create and looks just as good. Crown your table with a glamorous centrepiece such as a stunning vase of flowers or a low-hanging, glittering chandelier.

RIGHT The table is a market find that has been given a smart zinc top. On the table, a small blue cast-iron pot makes a funky vase.

FAR RIGHT Revive cupboards by painting doors in a rainbow of colours and give them chi-chi handles, as seen here.

OPPOSITE The dining room in the same house combines contemporary classics with antique finds. On the swanky boardroom-style chair is a cushion fashioned from a vintage Christian Dior scarf. On the 1970s table is an antique Indian pot with a single white flower.

THIS PAGE The sleek, chic kitchen in a London house shows how to mix retro style with modern lines. Without the beautiful candelabra in the corner and the painting – which takes its inspiration from an old silk scarf – this contemporary kitchen would simply lack spirit.

If you already have a sleek contemporary kitchen, you can adorn it with a handful of vintage flea-market finds to give it a little soul.

A country-style kitchen is particularly well suited to flea-market finds – right down to the kitchen sink (a butler sink, of course). For the walls, look for tongue-and-groove cladding, terracotta tiles or vintage floral wallpapers. For storage, choose freestanding pieces such as unpainted cupboards and old plate racks. Fabrics are an integral part of the country look, so scour markets for traditional country patterns (think floral, paisley or gingham) and fashion these pieces into tablecloths, curtains, tea towels or aprons. Create under-sink storage with a colourful curtain strung along a wire.

If you collect country-style kitchen accessories, make a display of them. Pieces of enamelware, collections of old copper pots, wooden chopping boards, handmade pottery, patterned plates, old coffee grinders and big copper kettles need to be showcased from like-minded shelves and cupboards such as old bookshelves, wardrobes with no doors and old laundry racks lashed to the ceiling.

Second-hand stoves and reconditioned ranges sometimes turn up at markets, but it pays to have such major fixtures overhauled and installed by a professional. An old shallow butler sink or deep Belfast sink accessorized with brass taps is another way to take your kitchen to the country.

For country-style eating spaces, start with a big, big table. You may find a large farmhouse or refectory table – or look for extendable pinewood tables or former boardroom tables to cover with a vintage tablecloth. For country-style seating, choose folding garden chairs, distressed painted chairs or an assortment of wooden chairs. Large benches, like big tables, bring people together, so look for old church pews or school benches to seat your dinner guests (soften hard edges with squab cushions covered in vintage fabrics).

ABOVE A plain backdrop allows for a subtle play of pattern and colour. The 1970s table is covered with floral vintage bark cloth.

OPPOSITE A pair of found bar stools transform a worktop into a breakfast bar. The antique silver cutlery is a collection of found single pieces, while the Moroccan tea glasses are a typical market find.

If you long to create a retro look, you need to go no further than your local market. You may be fortunate enough to unearth Formica-topped cupboards and sideboards from the 1950s as well as retro refrigerators. If not, many high street stores sell good reproductions, which you can easily accessorize with finds such as colourful melamine plates, cups and bowls, graphically decorated or pastel-coloured crockery, retro toasters and kettles, and kidney-shaped fruit bowls and vases. For a 1950s look, choose pieces in pastel. If it's a 1960s vibe that you're after, go for bold brassy colours (red, yellow, purple) and bold patterns.

LEFT An old tin makes a
beautiful container for
a bouquet of amaryllises.
This old farmhouse-style
table and its accompanying
quartet of ex-café chairs
are all classic market finds.

ABOVE Once used as a
hunting table in France,
this long thin table makes
a convivial dining spot. The
old school chairs, made
comfortable with cushions
sewn from vintage floral
fabrics, were cast-offs from
a local coffee-shop.

RIGHT The crowning
glory of this dining room
is an exquisite chandelier,
found in almost mint
condition at a market.
The antique mirror behind
reflects its beauty, turning
an ordinary space into
something extraordinary.

Markets will also furnish your retro dining space. Scour stalls for retro furniture pieces such as round plastic tables with matching moulded chairs, curvy wooden chairs and oval wooden tables. For total authenticity, serve drinks from a low-level wooden 1960s sideboard or wheel them in on a trolley. Clothe your table with tablecloths sewn from retro fabrics such as florals and candy stripes from the 1950s, graphic circles and swirls from the 1960s, or graphic fruit patterns from the 1970s.

Cooking and eating spaces are also happy to accommodate an eclectic look that consists of mismatched but beautiful objects. The common denominator will be your taste. While an all-out eclectic look can work (modern and classic, high tech with old tech), you may find that your own style falls into a new genre. Many markets are full of goods and food ideas from around the world, including chinoiserie tea caddies, tagine dishes, jade chopsticks, large Japanese soup bowls, Indian thali dishes and old French stewing pots.

Use your eye – and your tastebuds – to create your own eclectic look. 'Global ethnic', for example, might be reflected in a very simple and utilitarian cooking space with accessories such as Moroccan tea glasses, earthenware pots and Ethiopian coffee

pots, while the eating space is informal, focused on a low-level, Arabic-style table, with colourful cushions strewn all around. To create a low-level table, simply saw the legs off a taller one; to make your own cushion collection, sew antique Indian saris into covers for cushions for your guests to sit on. Source goods from local ethnic markets as well as markets you come across on your travels.

Whatever your style, flea markets will give you the opportunity to indulge your penchant for forgotten eating fashions. Revive fads such as 1970s fondue parties, cake decorating, pressure-cooking, coffee mornings, or the rituals of old-fashioned afternoon tea. You can serve tea out of bone-china cups and cake from a cake stand, find old lace doilies for plates and adorn your teapot with a knitted tea cosy.

THIS PAGE AND OPPOSITE This kitchen is full of otherworldly charm, its plain visage transformed with beautiful vintage things. Pieces of old wallpaper, antique postcards and sepia-toned photographs are stuck with masking tape to a perfectly ordinary fridge. The Belfast sink, the metal dish rack and the bentwood chairs add to its glamorous but careworn looks.

When it comes to shaping your cooking and eating areas, be honest about your needs. If you really do cook and eat on the run, then pick flea-market finds to suit your lifestyle as well as your style. If you live on your own but like to host the odd dinner party, choose flexible pieces, such as tables with drop leaves or slide-away leaves and fold-away chairs. If you live alone and eat out all the time, turn your back on a big cook–eat space and go for a breakfast-bar arrangement instead. Perch at a high bench on market-found bar stools or old laboratory stools. If TV dinners are your thing, look for breakfast trays, large coffee tables and low-level sofas so you can sit down, relax and feast on your takeaway in second-hand style.

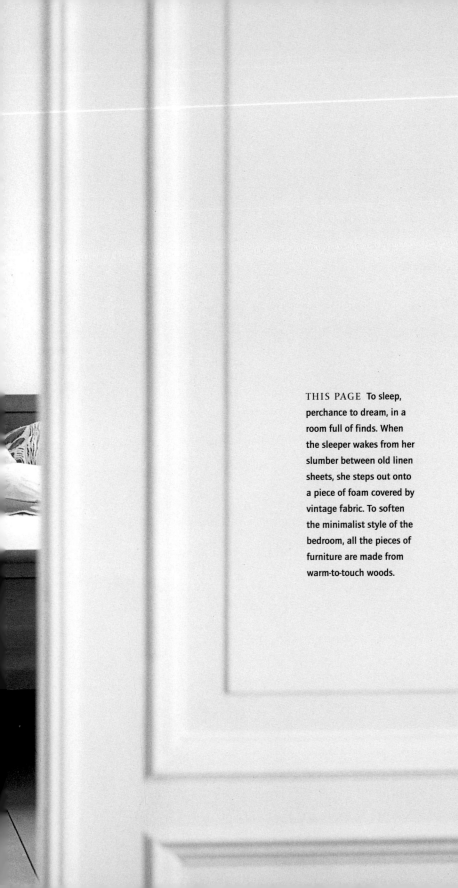

If you can't decide what style of bedroom you really want, keep an open mind and let the pieces you find at markets dictate the look.

THIS PAGE To sleep, perchance to dream, in a room full of finds. When the sleeper wakes from her slumber between old linen sheets, she steps out onto a piece of foam covered by vintage fabric. To soften the minimalist style of the bedroom, all the pieces of furniture are made from warm-to-touch woods.

sleeping spaces

Sleep the sleep of kings in your bedroom, and do it in second-hand style. While bedrooms are intimate spaces, they also say much about us as individuals – just walk into any bedroom and deduce from the style and state of the room what kind of person inhabits it. Markets can help you express yourself in your bedroom. And, in a bedroom styled to reflect just who you are, you can sleep easily.

Picture this. In your room is a headboard built out of an old gate, a rickety garden chair bought from a sunny Sunday village fair, and a cushion fashioned from a headscarf cherry-picked from a Paris flea market. Each individual item says so much about who you are and what you love. That's what makes your boudoir exclusive.

LEFT If you discover a beautiful bed frame but can't find a mattress to fit, you can do as this owner has done and fit a single divan within a queen-sized frame. The fabric on the bed and the valance are crafted from vintage fabrics, while the pillow is made from canvas sacking.

Special finds make most impact when they strike an unexpected pose. Hang a patchwork quilt on a wall, for example, or turn it into a makeshift curtain.

When it comes to arranging and furnishing your bedroom, there are some tried-and-tested styles to choose from. To save time and money, keep in mind the overall style that you are attempting to achieve, since this will influence your purchasing decisions. If you can't decide on a style, maintain an open mind and let the pieces you find dictate the look.

If you strike it lucky at a French market, for example, you may discover a beautiful *lit bateau* bed under dusty covers. With such an object as a room's centrepiece, you will naturally want to hunt down items to harmonize with its sassy style, such as a sparkly antique chandelier, heirloom linen sheets, a silk kimono or an ornate chaise longue.

A minimalist style is popular in bedrooms because there is something quietly relaxing about those pared-back lines and lack of clutter. To keep the space simple, all you need is a few big and beautiful things. The rest

ABOVE Pale bedding and furnishings give this small bedroom a spacious, light and airy feel. The curtain and the valance are from the same bolt of satin damask and add glamour.

LEFT Crisp white cotton pillowcases make a neutral contrast to this ethnic quilt. On the wall, family photos are mounted on bulldog clips attached to tiny pins. If you don't have enough photos of your own, you can buy albums from markets. A top hat is used as a desk tidy.

of the room can be left naked. Start by making neutral backdrops of the floors and walls (strict minimalists keep to white or off-white), but try to avoid creating too much starkness; you can soften the look with plenty of fabrics, using pattern and colour to magnetize the eye. One colourful silk cushion on a bed, for example, a cow hide on the floor or a white handmade lace shawl over the window is all you need to bring in warmth.

Unless you are lucky enough to have a separate dressing room, your bedroom will probably double as a dressing room. For lovers of minimalism, this means that efficient storage is vital. To create a streamlined space, you need to conceal clothes and accessories in one enormous wardrobe, painted in simple colours or left in its natural garb. Oversized

THIS PAGE Why buy a big lumbering wardrobe when you can hide your clothes behind curtains made from vintage fabrics? In this bedroom, other small clothing items are stowed under a bed in deep wooden trays that have been repainted in funky colours and given handles. The look here is East-meets-West, where traditional floral duvets are teamed with oriental paper lampshades.

THIS PAGE The clever-storage story continues. On an old strip of panelling fashioned into a shelf sit capacious bags that were found at an Indian market. Decapitated Indian tins have been stuck onto the wall to provide peep-show bedside shelving for books and ornaments.

wardrobes – and often crafted from beautiful old
hardwoods such as oak, mahogany and cherry –
turn up regularly at markets because many new
owners banish these from their homes in favour of
contemporary-style floor-to-ceiling storage. When
choosing a bed, look for one stunning piece with
a plain or ornate white headboard. Dress the bed
in light, airy, white neutrals, such as pure linen
sheets. While intact antique linens can be found at
many markets, you could also fashion your own
minimal-style duvet covers out of a patchwork of
white linen sheets.

There is something unpretentious and down-to-
earth about country style's soft, faded look that is
completely at home in bedrooms. A bedroom's star
is the bed, so choose from wrought-iron bedsteads,
old hospital beds and wooden beds to work this
look. Keep bed-frame paintwork in honest white or
leave it distressed.

When it comes to clothing your bed, there are
plenty of rustic choices, from floral duvet covers to
crochet patchwork blankets and old eiderdowns
with sateen covers. You can use eiderdowns as wall
hangings or window covers if they are exceptional
pieces. To revive an eiderdown, simply take it to
the dry-cleaner or hang it out on a washing line
in the sunlight for a day and follow up with a
shake and a good vacuum.

Like big floral dresses and Wellington boots,
patchwork has always been part of country-style
interiors. To create your own works, study old
patchwork quilts to see how many are sewn out of
scraps of clothes such as floral dresses, silk scarves,
tweed suit jackets, striped shirts and embroidered
baby clothes. When creating your own masterpiece,
scour vintage clothing markets for pieces like these,
but also keep your eyes open for conventional soft-

ABOVE Use texture to
soften pared-back lines in a
minimalist room. This plain
door, for example, has been
given a feminine twist with
its cover of flock wallpaper.
Show off your vintage
designer clothes against a
stark white backdrop.

RIGHT Every bed should
be well dressed. While the
trousers hanging over the
end of the bed may be this
year's Gucci, the beautiful
cushions are yesteryear's
silk scarves. Necklaces
strung from the bedhead
complete the outfit.

furnishing finds, such as striped cotton ticking,
gingham tablecloths and floral bedspreads. Instead
of duvet covers, you can clothe your bed with lovely
old woollen blankets, such as tartan rugs and ex-
army blankets. Country patterns – paisley, floral,
stripes and ginghams – can also be used to make
curtains, cushions and chair covers. If you want an
abundance of pattern, remember to avoid visual
overload by keeping the backdrop plain.

When it comes to storage, maintain the same
themes by choosing distressed wardrobes, painted

bookshelves and old wooden dressers. If you need alternative storage, use your country-style woven shopping bags, wicker hampers, tea chests and old suitcases. If you have room, consider acquiring an antique rocking chair, a wicker garden chair or a chocolate-brown leather armchair.

While bedrooms are designed for rest, they are also places for romance. Turn your room into a chic boudoir with pieces to please the senses. Create a come-hither space with tactile textures and seductive furnishings. While it is unlikely that you will find a four-poster bed at a market, you could build your own out of old boards, draping saris or silk scarves from the posts. Headboards are crucial to this look. Create your own by stretching a found fake animal skin across a length of board or restore an old rococo-style headboard. Create an air of luxury with too many pillows in an assortment of sizes and shapes. To complete the scene, put a

THIS PAGE Two single-bed finds have been joined to create one large bed. Two distinctive treasures – the ornate 1980s side lamp and the antique bedside cabinet – add a luxurious look to this loft bedroom.

THIS PAGE Import off-beat pieces into bedrooms to enhance character. In this room, a garden bench serves as a bedside table and an anglepoise desk light serves as a bedside lamp. A vintage tablecloth on the bed makes a chic alternative bedcover.

THIS PAGE A metal floral lamp, a vintage scarf draped over a lamp, an angel cookie cutter, and an open fan are just a few of the disparate things that, strangely, feel just right together in this calm, lived-in space. Plenty of white strikes a deal for peace with the multi-pattern mix.

classic piece of furniture alongside the bed, such as an old chaise longue or a Louis XVI-style armchair.

For a luxurious feel next to the skin, look for silk sheets at markets. For your bed cover, see if you can find velvet or velveteen curtains, popular in the 1980s, to fashion into oh-so-soft cushions or bedspreads. To complete this glamorous, sexy look, think lighting. Crown your room with one extravagantly large, low-hanging chandelier, or put gothic wall sconces above the bed instead of bedside lights. Pleasure seekers will ensure that

ABOVE Groovy bedroom, baby. This 1970s bed, with its headboard in the shape of car seats, is flanked by lengths of vintage floral fabrics to create the feel of an intimate four-poster in this airy warehouse. While you are running up the curtains, why not make a couple of skirts to rock around the house in, as this owner has done?

they get out of the right side of the bed each day by letting their feet step onto a sensuously soft rug – an old shag-pile carpet cut into a rug or a dyed sheepskin rug, for example.

If your style is more offbeat, seek out retro finds. Much of this particular quest is about discovering the right accessories, such as graphically decorated fabrics for bed covers, headboards, upholstery and cushions. Looks of the 1950s overlap a little with country style, which can be feminine at heart, especially if you go for the era's soft pastels – baby

pinks, pea greens and lemon yellows – combined with chintzy florals and paisleys. For a 1960s vibe, mix big graphic prints on soft furnishings derived from the vintage clothes, curtains and bedspreads. If pieces from the 1970s grab you, indulge your inner hippy and find a kaftan as a dressing gown, dress your bed in an Indian cotton bedspread and put a colourful dhurry on the floor.

For retro storage, search for low-level wooden sideboards. Instead of a conventional wardrobe, hide your clothes behind one large piece of vintage fabric strung up from a wire. If you are a collector of vintage clothes, why hide them at all? Display your prized pieces against a backdrop of white.

Alternatively, you can simply create your own look from flea-market discoveries by mixing and matching different styles and eras. Pieces used in unconventional ways – a side table crafted from a repainted stool, a fold-out garden chair covered in a lace scarf, an old school desk with the legs sawn off – make eye-catching statements. Use an old

sewing-machine trestle in place of a dressing table and find a Venetian-style mirror to lean against it.

Second-hand markets are also full of handy storage items, including good-quality coat-hangers, proper wooden suit-hangers, jewellery trinket boxes, hatboxes, shoehorns, shoe racks, lavender bags and large wicker laundry baskets. You will find yourself lingering over stalls of beautiful, memory-evoking items from the past, such as old photographs, Chinese fans, pinned butterflies, oil paintings and piles of vintage magazines. Any of these can be used to embellish your bedroom walls.

Once you have hunted down all the things that make you feel at home, curl up and go to sleep. After all, shopping is such hard work.

ABOVE LEFT **A brightly coloured patchwork blanket from a baby's cot adds a slash of visual interest to this minimalist bedroom. The curtain has been made by sewing together strips of vintage floral and striped fabrics.**

ABOVE **For a little luxury, track down an original kimono to swan around in, like the red one seen here. A pretty lace panel makes an eye-stopping, light-enhancing window cover.**

THIS PAGE If you uncover old bed ends like these, snap them up and fasten them to a modern bed. Cover any under-bed sins with a valance, which you can create from fabric bolts, tablecloths or old bedspreads. To show off finds, create a gallery 'space' such as these built-in cupboards, exhibited to a rhapsody in blue.

THIS PAGE Bathrooms should be relaxing places, devoted to the revival and refreshment of body and soul. From the gentle, off-white colour scheme to the market-found accessories – a tin-saucer soap dish, a former living-room mirror and an ethnic wooden stool – everything in this room is conducive to calm.

RIGHT Every bathroom
needs a mirror, so, if you
come across one whose
shape you like but whose
frame is dull, all you need
to do is to repaint it.

Bathrooms are intimate and
sensual spaces – one of the
few really private places in
the home – so make them
yours with things you love.

bathing
spaces

Traditionally, bathrooms have been treated as an
afterthought in the design and decoration of a
home. Unlike kitchens and living rooms, they are
private, intimate spaces, often tucked away in dark,
pint-sized rooms. While bathrooms are primarily
functional, we are now demanding that they should
also be havens of peace, so that we can soothe
away all our cares behind their closed doors.

That is where flea-market style comes in. The
items that can be found at markets – large rolltop
baths, large Victorian shower-rose heads, antique
mirrors – all look beautiful, extolling a careworn,
lived-in look. And, while it is important to get your
bathroom's functional elements right, the pieces

you will pick up at markets will help you to get the
aesthetics right so that you can use your steamy
sanctuary for genuine, deep relaxation.

Start with the room's backdrops, the floors and
walls. Many bathrooms are located in the smallest,
darkest rooms in the home. If this is true in your
case, use optical illusion to make the space seem
bigger. To 'create' space, you need to maximize the
light in the room, so make large surfaces glossy
and the overall colour scheme light and bright.

The need for lightness extends to floors, which
can be covered with reclaimed tiles or lengths of
pale antique timbers. The shinier the floor, the
more light it will reflect, so coat your timber in a

THIS PAGE With its pink, blue and white colour scheme, the overall look of this room is peaceful and reassuring. The candy-coloured, woven-plastic chair is both attractive and waterproof. A former magazine rack provides bathside reading storage.

THIS PICTURE A glass-fronted cabinet repainted in a tranquil blue is filled with quirky, witty objects for the bather to admire. Its mirrored back reflects light around the room and enhances the feeling of space in the room.

ABOVE LEFT At the end of the day, nothing is more soothing on the eye than the soft, warm light of candles. These ones stand in old enamel lamplighters.

LEFT This crocheted rug and vintage vest are common market finds, which provide handy post-bath wear. Laundry often ends up in bathrooms so tidy it into a container like the string bag seen here.

THIS PICTURE Built-in bath surrounds don't have to be boring. This one has been given a facelift with vintage fabric, which has then been sprayed with shoe waterproofing. As an alternative, you could use waterproof wallpaper or PVC-style tablecloths. Instead of residing in its ugly sister of a plastic container, the bubble bath has been decanted into an old vodka bottle.

glossy varnish. Linoleum, currently back in vogue, is one of those floorings many people strip out of their new homes in favour of more contemporary floor coverings, but the good news for finders is that lino is a hard-wearing, splash-proof, child-friendly flooring. If you can't find enough to cover your floor, simply cut off a strip to use as a mat in areas prone to splashes and spills.

When you step out of your luxurious bath, you will want to step onto a bathmat that is kind to the soles of your feet. It is possible to find mats made from original duckboard slats, old shag-pile towelling or cork. Alternatively, make one from a thick towel or a piece of carpet – or use a rug.

White tiles are functional and beautiful on walls. Even if you opt for new tiles, keep your eyes open for off-beat second-hand tiles to break up the too-smooth look of new tiles. For example, you could create a patchwork of old white-and-blue Delft tiles (often stripped out of Victorian bathrooms) or add a strip of colourful Moroccan mosaic tiles. For a rustic feel, clad your walls in reclaimed wood.

A bathroom wall's ornaments are its mirrors. While you need mirrors for daily bathroom rituals, you can also, by strategic positioning, use them to harness the spatial powers of light. If you find a mirror that's the right shape but has an ugly frame, simply repaint the frame in a colour to suit your room or make one yourself out of natural objects such as found sea-shells, sand-coloured pebbles or driftwood. If you have limited wall space, you could give wall-mounted bathroom cabinets a shiny new mirrored face to help enhance the light.

The centrepiece of most bathrooms is, of course, the bath. One of the most popular fixtures, which brings with it an air of luxury and indulgence, is an antique cast-iron, claw-footed, rolltop bath. If you

seat. For a bathroom with a sense of humour, dress your lavatory in a kitsch, colourful towelling seat cover and paint the outside of the bath and the cupboard below the basin in contrasting colours.

If there is enough room, other pieces of furniture can be used to add to the feeling of repose, such as generously large armchairs, chaise longues or daybeds. Apart from adding to the comfort and luxury of the room, such seating makes it easier to carry out beauty routines such as pedicures and facials. Small tables, such as former coffee tables

LEFT A gallery of mirrors in all shapes and sizes creates an eye-catching display to maximize light from the skylight above.

BELOW The initial 'E' and the collections of old postcards add a personal touch to a small bathroom. For an air freshener with a natural difference, drill holes into a block of wood and burn earthy incense.

Give a new bath character with a cladding of vintage wallpaper, reclaimed timber or a patchwork of old tiles.

find a bath whose enamel is chipped or cracked, you can get it re-enamelled, but bear in mind that this can double a bath's original price. Look for reconditioned taps and spout fittings, which should be installed by a professional plumber. If you find a bath with broken legs, simply remount it on slats of antique reclaimed timber or breeze blocks.

Even in a bathroom, flea-market style defies tradition. If you shun the idea of a conventional matching three-piece suite, your bathroom could be a happy mismatch of reclaimed bathtub, basin and lavatory. You could marry an old copper tub with a Victorian lavatory and a washstand backed with old tiles, or combine a rolltop tub with a Belfast sink and a lavatory with a reclaimed mahogany

THIS PAGE A calm display to bathe by is dominated by an empty picture frame and a picture of a nude with downcast eyes, both sitting alongside dishes, blocky vases and an heirloom candle-holder on a wooden work bench.

OPPOSITE This room is full of beautiful finds: the 'tables' (wooden crates resting on their ends), the Belfast sink with antique taps and the glamorous, necklace-draped mirror.

or wrought-iron garden tables, provide surfaces for stacks of towels, fresh flowers or your collection of lotions and potions.

For total relaxation, the view from the bathtub needs to be uncluttered, so make it possible to keep everything tidied away by installing ample storage. You will find former bathroom cabinets at markets and you can import other storage ideas from around the home. Pile your towels into old wardrobes or chests of drawers, and house your toiletries and elixirs in old medical cabinets or an unused bedside drawer.

When it comes to small storage, market finds and their uses are infinite. You can, for example, use old pails or topless olive-oil cans as waste bins and put your toothbrushes in vintage vases or old coloured-glass tumblers. Pile lavatory rolls in old shopping baskets or hatboxes and use sculptural ashtrays and delicate china saucers as soap dishes.

Old grooming items sometimes turn up at markets, including manicure sets, hand mirrors, eyelash curlers, bone-handled hairbrushes, curlers and shaver brushes. These implements are often sturdy and built to last, and do the job much better than their flimsy contemporary counterparts.

With all your clutter swept away, the next thing is to evoke a calm, peaceful atmosphere. A small posy of flowers in an old china tea cup or a leafy green plant in an old chamber pot will give you something living and breathing to look at. You can also bring yourself back to earth with finds from nature, such as coral florets, conch shells, fossil swirls and pieces of sculptural driftwood.

The flickering, warm light of a flame is soft on tired eyes so, for an ultra-soothing effect, transform your bathroom at night into a grotto of candles. Place your candles in old storm lanterns, elegant

oil lamps or graceful antique candelabra, or dot tealights in Moroccan tea glasses around the room.

To enhance your privacy, use beautiful window coverings to exclude prying eyes while maintaining an aesthetically pleasing look. To let light diffuse through the curtains, source pieces such as lace shawls and linen tablecloths, or create a patchwork curtain from old silk scarves in pale colours.

ABOVE A shower alcove has been tiled with second-hand tiles and accessorized with vintage towels.

RIGHT A sauna-like feel has been created in this bathroom by the use of reclaimed wood.

THIS PICTURE What was originally a hospital cot has been sprayed with colourful paints to give it a new lease of life. While it's easy to indulge your inner child, try to avoid colour overdrive. Remember that bedrooms are where your children unwind and relax. Use plenty of white space to strike a balance.

When it comes to decorating your child's bedroom, flea-market style says, 'Come on, let's play.' There's something about finding furniture for children's rooms that allows us to let our inner child have free rein.

children's spaces

Children's spaces are their studies and bedrooms – or, if you are lucky, a separate rumpus room. In most cases, children's play areas spill into parents' living areas, so, to keep the rising tide of primary-coloured toys at bay, good storage is vital. To keep your own living space looking sane, hunt for finds such tea chests, trunks, suitcases, wicker baskets and laundry baskets that will fit in with your décor.

In your child's bedroom, however, you can let your hair down. It is a good idea to keep walls and floors neutral since children's tastes change like the wind. Let today's favourite pictures and posters of cartoons, animals and pop stars blow in and out onto blank spaces. The overall feel should be

a relaxed one since the bedroom is where a child unwinds. Children love bright colour schemes, but temper loud colours with plenty of deep contrasts and gentle, harmonious tones.

When buying bedroom furniture, there are plenty of beds to pick from, including wrought-iron cots, old hospital beds and bassinets. If you are buying a cot or bassinet for a young baby, it is advisable to buy a new mattress for reasons of good hygiene.

Scour markets for small chests of drawers; if you find a painted chest, you can always strip it and repaint it in your child's favourite colour. Children who can dress themselves will love having storage that is easy to access, so put their clothes in big

ABOVE If you find an old armchair in reasonable condition, customize it for a children's bedroom by re-upholstering it in colourful thick fabrics or sewing a loose cover. Take home waifs and strays like this floppy-eared bunny.

THIS PAGE Create a patchwork of patterns on a bed. Here striped pillow cases, floral pillow covers and chinoiserie-style sheets combine to make an eye-catching mélange.

OPPOSITE Irresistible eye-candy for a little girl, the wall behind the wardrobe is a collage of wallpaper scraps, collected from ends of rolls, pattern books and swatch samples.

coloured shopping baskets or sturdy cardboard boxes covered in wallpaper remnants or gift wrap. A small reclaimed wardrobe is always handy, but, if your child likes choosing his or her own clothes, you could string up a washing line or fasten a pole between two solid wooden posts nailed to the wall to make a small-scale open wardrobe.

For bedroom chairs, re-upholster or create covers for second-hand armchairs from colourful, sturdy vintage-textile finds such as canvas, ticking fabrics, former curtains and bedspreads. Or accessorize a plain armchair with brightly coloured cushion covers adapted from vintage fabrics such as old scarves, aprons and dresses.

Cover your child's bed in colourful finds such as crocheted rugs or patchwork duvets, or dye plain cot blankets. Making a patchwork bedcover for an adult's bed is daunting, but creating a patchwork throw from vintage finds for a baby's cot is less of a challenge; you can always add on bits as your baby moves from bassinet to cot to single bed. Old children's clothes, particularly those incorporating bits of embroidery, lacework or prints, are an ideal starting point for a patchwork cover. One natural

LEFT Hand-me-downs like these children's chairs often end up in markets when they get to the end of the line; in this case, all that was needed was a new coat of paint. Children like things with a sense of fun, such as the blow-up beach balls and globes hung from the ceiling. Look out for mural-sized artworks like this Russian scene, which absorbs children for hours.

RIGHT Take some of the work out of homework by giving your children a bright and sunny place to study. In this room, a 1970s-style storage system is used to tidy away pens, pencils, rulers and other stationery. For a study light, a rusty anglepoise lamp has been sprayed with cherry-red gloss paint, and an old typist's chair has been repainted buttery yellow.

ABOVE Open shelving has been transformed into a zoo for stuffed animals. Covered in old pieces of wrapping paper and scraps of vintage wallpaper, it is a visual feast for tiny eyes.

ABOVE Old coat hooks, painted duck-egg blue, make an open showcase for a vintage hand-knitted child's coat, which is displayed on a kitsch crocheted coat hanger.

ABOVE An ordinary chest of drawers looks pretty in its new pink coat. The elephant on top is made out of a vintage towel; the gaudy gilt ornament beside it has become a flower pot.

Children love bright colour schemes, but temper loud colours with deep contrasts and gentle, harmonious tones.

fabric that is kind and gentle on young children's skin is linen. If you find antique linen sheets, simply cut them up to cot sizes and dye them.

Good storage in children's bedrooms is essential, especially if your child is a natural magpie. Most children also like to see their belongings, so try to mix open storage with chests, boxes or suitcases. For open shelving, reuse old bookshelves.

No matter how hard you try to resist, you will find that you often go to a market with your own must-get shopping list and return with a collection of orphaned toys. Second-hand finds usually cost half the amount of shop-bought ones and, given

the fickleness of children's affections, buying from markets means that you won't have spent a fortune on something that is loved only for five minutes.

While markets offer plenty of yesterday's toys – old tin soldiers, stuffed animals, rocking horses and Russian dolls – you will also find a huge array of grown-up playthings and knick-knacks that children adore: old trinket boxes, perfume bottles, garden gnomes, sea shells, cowboy hats, garlands – you name it. If you are brave, take your child along with you to a second-hand market and see it from their perspective. If you get them to enjoy shopping from markets at an early age, they'll love it for life.

THIS PAGE Instead of a conventional chest of drawers, reclaim an old desk and paint it a vibrant colour. The beautiful old Danish wooden cot is clothed in vintage fabric cushions and patchwork and woollen blankets.

LEFT Former industrial pieces – such as the low-hanging factory lights, the long factory table (with its gorgeous customized legs) and the wall of paper-filing cabinets – suit a former industrial space. Around the table is a collection of ex-office seats and factory chairs with swivel bases.

While some simply need a space to study, write letters and pay bills, for more and more of us the home office is our workplace.

work spaces

Tailor-made second-hand items for work spaces at home generally come from their original habitats: offices. Some pieces do turn up at markets, but office liquidation sales, office furniture auctions and second-hand office furniture outlets are often more fruitful picking grounds.

Office desks, available in various configurations, are ideal for the job for which they were designed. If a desk is too corporate in appearance, replace its pinstriped suit with a colourful coat of paint or hide it under an old tablecloth. If the desk has drawers, consider painting each drawer a different colour or giving the drawers a new set of knobs.

Early examples of desks, such as large rolltop desks, often come with plenty of built-in storage. Sometimes 'working' tables, built for long hours of labour – architects' drawing boards, leather-and-fabric cutting tables, factory assembly tables and antique sewing-machine trestles (*sans* machine) – turn up at markets when warehouses are stripped out, but tables that are more commonly found, such as old school desks, small pine dining tables and glass-topped tables, work equally well.

Another solution is to make your own. For a cheap chic desk, rest a plain door on two support pillars such as towers of bricks, wooden trestles, bedside drawers or a duo of filing cabinets.

A good chair is essential. If you will be spending a lot of time at your desk, choose one that gives you adequate support. Try your chair before you buy it and remember the rules: your feet should be firmly planted on the floor (if they don't reach, a foot-rest of second-hand books or an old winebox will do); your lower back must be well supported; and your arms must be at right angles to the desktop. Consider acquiring a typist's chair, which will be fully adjustable and ergonomically designed to support your posture. Give your chair a new personality by re-upholstering the seat and backrest in funky vintage-fabric finds.

Other chairs, such as leather boardroom chairs, architects' stools, school chairs and simple wooden

RIGHT Metal cabinets can be easily painted or stripped, but an original colour like this looks just right in this industrial-style room with its backdrop of painted brickwork. Pens, rulers and paintbrushes are stored on top of the cabinet in vases, tin cups, old mugs and bottles.

THIS PAGE There are all sorts of ways to fashion a desk. Here, old wooden trestles are crowned with a shiny new reinforced-glass top. Instead of cushions to soften the seat of a chair, simply use a folded-up rug. The table lamp, with its odd pairing of long, elegant base and frumpy shade, looks eccentric.

THIS PAGE Industrial-look discoveries are brought together here to create a hard-working work station. Factory finds such as the desk, chair and metal shelving unit often surface at markets. On the desk is the perfect personal lighting assistant: a draughtsman's lamp.

chairs will also serve your desk well. If you need to adjust a chair to your height, shorten its legs with a saw or put a squab on the seat.

Every work space needs a light designed with reading in mind, and there is nothing to beat the adjustable anglepoise desk light (but check the joints and springs to ensure they are not too stiff or saggy). Small bedside reading lamps or large floor lamps also throw out plenty of light.

In addition to office storage, most of us require some kind of filing system for keeping our personal papers in order. Office furniture will do the job well, but may need customizing to fit in with a particular room's décor. Other storage ideas include old postal shelves, chests of drawers, old metal gym lockers, old bookshelves, doorless wardrobes and, for files, plate racks nailed to walls.

To keep your desk tidy, unearth something to suit your second-hand style rather than the usual plastic desk tidy more commonly spotted in low-ceilinged offices with grey walls. Store your pens,

OPPOSITE PAGE This work corner, sectioned off with a patchwork of silk scarves, is home to a rolltop desk, complete with its own storage.

LEFT You can find a work niche like this one in 'dead' space beside the stairs. Here an industrial light is attached to the side of the staircase, lighting a former printing-factory desk.

ABOVE This tiny work space is shoehorned into a living-room corner. An ex-postal cabinet gives plenty of storage for paperwork.

pencils, rulers and scissors in vintage vases, milk jugs, old tins, tea caddies, jam jars – whatever you can find. Builders' plastic odds-'n'-ends boxes – which are normally reserved for housing nails and screws – are ideal for staples, paperclips, erasers and pencil sharpeners.

Markets often reveal other early examples of desk accessories, including old Bakelite phones, quills and inkpots, kitsch paperweights, antique typewriters and bone-handled paper knives.

For storing notepads, staplers, hole-punchers and CDs, buy larger containers such as antique leather suitcases, jewellery chests, and hatboxes or cardboard shoeboxes jazzed up with vintage wallpaper or wrapping paper.

sources

Whether you are a self-confessed flea-market addict or are simply browsing with your family, there are plenty of flea-market-style shopping opportunities at home and away.

To find the best hunting grounds, look in local papers and on public noticeboards for old-fashioned jumble sales, garage sales and car-boot sales. Smaller local markets often have bric-à-brac stalls, as do church, village and school fêtes. Visit local antique shops, charity shops, auctions and architectural salvage yards. Keep your eyes open for interesting-looking skips. If you are in France, locate the nearest *brocante*, often housed in a church or village hall.

For larger antique and collectors' markets, and European and American flea markets, surf the internet to check dates and locations. The internet also hosts a wealth of antique and auctioneering sites, providing plenty of opportunities for international purchases.

IN THE UK

LONDON

Most street markets have a few bric-à-brac stalls, but here is a list of established London locations specializing in antiques and second-hand items. Consult websites for seasonal opening hours. For general information on street markets in London, visit *www.streetsensation. co.uk/markets*.

Portobello
Portobello Road, London W11
Friday and Saturday, 8am to 5pm
www.portobelloroad.co.uk

Brick Lane
Brick Lane, Cheshire Street and Sclater Street, London E1 and E2
Sunday, 6am to 1pm
www.eastlondonmarkets.com

Bermondsey
Bermondsey Square, London SE1
Friday, 5am to 1pm

Camden
Camden High Street, London NW1
Saturday and Sunday, 9am to 5pm, and most weekdays
www.camdenlock.net

Greenwich
Greenwich Church Street, Stockwell Street and Greenwich High Road, London SE10
Saturday and Sunday, 9.30am to 5pm
www.greenwich-market.co.uk

OUTSIDE LONDON

Among regular antique fairs are those at Newark (Notts), Swinderby (Lincs), Ardingly (East Sussex) and Goodwood (West Sussex). Consult the following websites for more information: *www.antiques-atlas.com* and *www.artefact.co.uk*. For architectural salvage, consult *www.salvoweb.com*

AROUND EUROPE

For general information on flea markets and a comprehensive list of links, consult *www.fleamarket.com*.

FRANCE
www.discoverfrance.net

Puces de Clignancourt
Rue des Entrepots, Saint Ouen, 75018 Paris
Saturday, Sunday, Monday
www.parispuces.com

Puces de Montreuil
Avenue de la Porte de Montreuil, 75020 Paris
Saturday, Sunday, Monday

BELGIUM

For information on antiques and flea markets in Belgium, consult *www.visitbelgium.com*

DENMARK

For information on flea markets, auction houses and antiques in Copenhagen and surrounding areas, visit *www.woko.dk*. Another good site for second-hand shops and flea markets is *www.useit.dk*.

THE NETHERLANDS

The Netherlands' largest second-hand event is on 30 April, when the whole of Amsterdam turns into one huge flea market! The areas of Noordermarkt and Waterlooplein also host regular good markets – visit tourist offices in the city or look on the internet for details.

IN THE USA

For comprehensive state-by-state flea-market directories, visit *www.fleausa.com* and *www.fleamarketguide.com*. For indispensable flea-market inspiration, visit *www.carterjunk.com*, a site for the true flea-market devotee.

NEW YORK
'The Annex'/the 26th street flea
Sixth Avenue and West 26th Street, New York
Saturday and Sunday, sunrise to sunset

ON THE WEB

The internet has numerous auction sites, enabling global shopping and giving access to a pool of unusual items. One of the best known and comprehensive of these sites is *www.ebay.com*.

picture credits

All photography by Debi Treloar.

key **a**=above, **b**=below, **r**=right, **l**=left, **c**=centre.

Endpapers Story; **page 1** designer Petra Boase & family's home in Norfolk; **2** designer Susanne Rutzou's home in Copenhagen; **3** Debi Treloar's home in London; **4** Sigolène Prébois of Tsé &Tsé associées home in Paris; **5** Catherine Lévy of Tsé &Tsé associées home in Paris; **12–13** author, stylist and Caravan (shop) owner Emily Chalmers and director Chris Richmond's home in London; **14** owner of Crème de la Crème à la Edgar, Helle Høgsbro Krag's home in Copenhagen; **15 inset** Debi Treloar's home in London; **16a** owners of Maisonette, Martin Barrell & Amanda Sellers' home in London; **16bl** Debi Treloar's home in London; **16br** the home in Copenhagen of producer Samina Langholz of Bullet Productions (www.bullet.dk); **17** Debi Treloar's home in London; **18** & **19r** owners of Maisonette, Martin Barrell & Amanda Sellers' home in London; **19l** designer Susanne Rutzou's home in Copenhagen; **20a** Sigolène Prébois of Tsé &Tsé associées home in Paris; **20b** the Philadelphia home of Glen Senk & Keith Johnson of Anthropologie; **21** Anita Calero; **22–23** designer Susanne Rutzou's home in Copenhagen; **24al** the Philadelphia home of Kristin Norris, creative director at Anthropologie, and Trevor Lunn, digital designer; **24bl** Catherine Lévy of Tsé &Tsé associées home in Paris; **24r** & **25** owner of Crème de la Crème à la Edgar, Helle Høgsbro Krag's home in Copenhagen; **26** Debi Treloar's home in London; **27 background** the Chestnut Hill home of Pamela Falk; **27 inset** designer Petra Boase & family's home in Norfolk; **28** owners of Maisonette, Martin Barrell & Amanda Sellers' home in London; **28 inset** Debi Treloar's home in London; **29**, **30** & **31l** author, stylist and Caravan (shop) owner Emily Chalmers and director Chris Richmond's home in London; **31r** Debi Treloar's home in London; **32al** designer Susanne Rutzou's home in Copenhagen; **32ar** the Philadelphia home of Kristin Norris, creative director at Anthropologie, and Trevor Lunn, digital designer; **32b** the Philadelphia home of Glen Senk & Keith Johnson of Anthropologie; **33l** designer Susanne Rutzou's home in Copenhagen; **33r** Story; **34 both** designer Petra Boase & family's home in Norfolk; **35–36** Debi Treloar's home in London; **37l** the home in Copenhagen of producer Samina Langholz of Bullet Productions (www.bullet.dk); **37r both** designer Petra Boase & family's home in Norfolk; **38–39** designer Susanne Rutzou's home in Copenhagen; **39bl** the Philadelphia home of Glen Senk & Keith Johnson of Anthropologie; **39ar** the home in Copenhagen of producer Samina Langholz of Bullet Productions (www.bullet.dk); **40** the guesthouse of the interior designer & artist Philippe Guilmin, Brussels; **40 inset** & **41** owner of Crème de la Crème à la Edgar, Helle Høgsbro Krag's home in Copenhagen; **42** the home in Copenhagen of producer Samina Langholz of Bullet Productions (www.bullet.dk); **43** the guesthouse of the interior designer & artist Philippe Guilmin, Brussels; **44** owners of Maisonette, Martin Barrell & Amanda Sellers' home in London; **45bl**&**ar** designer Susanne Rutzou's home in Copenhagen; **45c** owner of Crème de la Crème à la Edgar, Helle Høgsbro Krag's home in Copenhagen; **46** the home in Copenhagen of producer Samina Langholz of Bullet Productions (www.bullet.dk); **47bl** designer Susanne Rutzou's home in Copenhagen; **47ar** owner of Crème de la Crème à la Edgar, Helle Høgsbro Krag's home in Copenhagen; **48al** the home in Copenhagen of producer Samina Langholz of Bullet Productions (www.bullet.dk); **48bl**, **48ar** & **49** the guesthouse of the interior designer & artist Philippe Guilmin, Brussels; **50** author, stylist and Caravan (shop) owner Emily Chalmers and director Chris Richmond's home in London; **51l** Debi Treloar's home in London; **51r both** Catherine Lévy of Tsé &Tsé associées home in Paris; **52** the Chestnut Hill home of Pamela Falk; **53 inset** the Chestnut Hill home of Pamela Falk; **54** the guesthouse of the interior designer & artist Philippe Guilmin, Brussels; **55 main** the guesthouse of the interior designer & artist Philippe Guilmin, Brussels; **55 inset** designer Steven Shailer's apartment in New York City; **56 main** Catherine Lévy of Tsé &Tsé associées home in Paris; **56 inset** designer Petra Boase & family's home in Norfolk; **57l** Debi Treloar's home in London; **57r** the home in Copenhagen of producer Samina Langholz of Bullet Productions (www.bullet.dk); **58l** owners of Maisonette, Martin Barrell & Amanda Sellers' home in London; **58r** Debi Treloar's home in London; **59** Sigolène Prébois of Tsé &Tsé associées home in Paris; **60** John Derian's apartment in New York; **61c** Anita Calero; **61bl** Catherine Lévy of Tsé &Tsé associées home in Paris; **61br** the home in Copenhagen of producer Samina Langholz of Bullet Productions (www.bullet.dk); **62al** the Philadelphia home of Glen Senk & Keith Johnson of Anthropologie; **62bl** owner of Crème de la Crème à la Edgar, Helle Høgsbro Krag's home in Copenhagen; **62ar** John Derian's apartment in New York; **62br** the Chestnut Hill home of Pamela Falk; **63l** the Philadelphia home of Glen Senk & Keith Johnson of Anthropologie; **63r** designer Steven Shailer's apartment in New York City; **64 all** designer Susanne Rutzou's home in Copenhagen; **65 inset** Anita Calero; **65 main** designer Susanne Rutzou's home in Copenhagen; **66al** & **bc** Catherine Lévy of Tsé &Tsé associées home in Paris; **66ar** & **67** author, stylist and Caravan (shop) owner Emily Chalmers and director Chris Richmond's home in London; **68–69** all Story except **68ar inset** owners of Maisonette, Martin Barrell & Amanda Sellers' home in London; **70–71 all** Catherine Lévy of Tsé &Tsé associées home in Paris except **70ar** the Philadelphia home of Kristin Norris, creative director at Anthropologie, and Trevor Lunn, digital designer; **72–73** the home in Copenhagen of producer Samina Langholz of Bullet Productions (www.bullet.dk); **74–75** author, stylist and Caravan (shop) owner Emily Chalmers and director Chris Richmond's home in London; **76–77** the home in Copenhagen of producer Samina Langholz of Bullet Productions (www.bullet.dk); **78** designer Susanne Rutzou's home in Copenhagen; **79** owners of Maisonette, Martin Barrell & Amanda Sellers' home in London; **80** the guesthouse of the interior designer & artist Philippe Guilmin, Brussels; **81** owner of Crème de la Crème à la Edgar, Helle Høgsbro Krag's home in Copenhagen; **82b** John Derian's apartment in New York; **82a** designer Steven Shailer's apartment in New York City; **83** Anita Calero; **84** the Philadelphia home of Glen Senk & Keith Johnson of Anthropologie; **85** the Philadelphia home of Kristin Norris, creative director at Anthropologie, and Trevor Lunn, digital designer; **86** Story; **87** Debi Treloar's home in London; **88–89** Catherine Lévy of Tsé &Tsé associées home in Paris; **90–91** the guesthouse of the interior designer & artist Philippe Guilmin, Brussels; **92** the Philadelphia home of Kristin Norris, creative director at Anthropologie, and Trevor Lunn, digital designer; **93 all** Sigolène Prébois of Tsé &Tsé associées home in Paris; **94–95** owners of Maisonette, Martin Barrell & Amanda Sellers' home in London; **96–97** Debi Treloar's home in London; **98** John Derian's apartment in New York; **98–99** author, stylist and Caravan (shop) owner Emily Chalmers and director Chris Richmond's home in London; **99** owner of Crème de la Crème à la Edgar, Helle Høgsbro Krag's home in Copenhagen; **100–101 all** Story; **102–103** designer Susanne Rutzou's home in Copenhagen; **104l** the Philadelphia home of Glen Senk & Keith Johnson of Anthropologie; **104–105** the Chestnut Hill home of Pamela Falk; **105** John Derian's apartment in New York; **106–107** Catherine Lévy of Tsé &Tsé associées home in Paris; **108–109** owners of Maisonette, Martin Barrell & Amanda Sellers' home in London; **110** owner of Crème de la Crème à la Edgar, Helle Høgsbro Krag's home in Copenhagen; **111** the guesthouse of the interior designer & artist Philippe Guilmin, Brussels; **112** designer Petra Boase & family's home in Norfolk; **113** author, stylist and Caravan (shop) owner Emily Chalmers and director Chris Richmond's home in London; **114r** the home in Copenhagen of producer Samina Langholz of Bullet Productions (www.bullet.dk); **114l, 115** & **116** Debi Treloar's home in London; **117–19** designer Petra Boase & family's home in Norfolk; **120** & **121r** author, stylist and Caravan (shop) owner Emily Chalmers and director Chris Richmond's home in London; **121l** Sigolène Prébois of Tsé &Tsé associées home in Paris; **122** the guesthouse of the interior designer & artist Philippe Guilmin, Brussels; **123** Story; **124–25** the guesthouse of the interior designer & artist Philippe Guilmin, Brussels; **126** Sigolène Prébois of Tsé &Tsé associées home in Paris; **127** designer Petra Boase & family's home in Norfolk; **128–29** Debi Treloar's home in London; **130** Sigolène Prébois of Tsé &Tsé associées home in Paris; **131–33** owner of Crème de la Crème à la Edgar, Helle Høgsbro Krag's home in Copenhagen; **134–35** the guesthouse of the interior designer & artist Philippe Guilmin, Brussels; **136** John Derian's apartment in New York; **137** the Philadelphia home of Glen Senk & Keith Johnson of Anthropologie; **138** author, stylist and Caravan (shop) owner Emily Chalmers and director Chris Richmond's home in London; **139b** Sigolène Prébois of Tsé &Tsé associées home in Paris; **139a** designer Steven Shailer's apartment in New York City.

business credits

Anita Calero Photography

521 West 23rd Street # 6R
New York, NY 10011
USA
+ 1 212 727 8949
www.apostrophe.net
Pages 21, 61c, 65 inset, 83.

Anthropologie

+ 1 800 309 2500
www.anthropologie.com
*Pages 20b, 24al, 32ar, 32b, 39bl, 62al, 63l,
70ar, 84, 85, 92, 104l, 137.*

Bois-Renard

Decorative home accessories
+ 1 215 247 4777
*Pages 27 background, 52, 53 inset, 62br,
104–105.*

Bullet Productions

www.bullet.dk
*Pages 16br, 37l, 39ar, 42, 46, 48al, 57r, 61br,
72–73, 76–77, 114r.*

Crème de la Crème à la Edgar

Kompagnistræde 8,st
1208 Copenhagen K
Denmark
+ 45 33361818
*Pages 14, 24r, 25, 40 inset, 41 , 45c, 47ar, 62bl,
81, 99, 110, 131–33.*

Debi Treloar

www.debitreloar.com
*Pages 3, 15 inset, 16bl, 17, 26, 28 inset, 31r,
35–36, 51l, 57l, 58r, 87, 96–97, 114l, 115,
116, 128–29.*

Emily Chalmers

author & stylist
www.emilychalmers.com
Caravan
11 Lamb Street
Spitalfields
London E1 6EA
020 7247 6467
www.caravanstyle.com
*Pages 12–13, 29, 30, 31l, 50, 66ar, 67, 74–75,
98–99, 113, 120, 121r, 138.*

John Derian

store
6 East 2nd Street
New York, NY 10003
USA
+ 1 212 677 3917
www.johnderian.com
Pages 60, 62ar, 82b, 98, 105, 136

Maisonette

020 8964 8444
maisonette.uk@aol.com
www.maisonette.uk.com
For location booking, please call Richard
Smith at InSpace 07050 189 375.
*Pages 16a, 18, 19r, 28, 44, 58l, 68ar, 79,
94–95, 108–109.*

Petra Boase

www.petraboase.com
info@petraboase.com
*Pages 1, 27 inset, 34 both, 37r, 56 inset, 112,
117–19, 127.*

Philippe Guilmin

interior designer & artist
philippe.guilmin@skynet.be
*Pages 40, 43, 48bl, 48ar, 49, 54, 55 main, 80,
90–91, 111, 122, 124–25, 134–35.*

Rützou A/S

+ 45 35240616
www.rutzou.com
cph@rutzou.com
*Pages 2, 19l, 22–23, 32al, 33l, 38–39, 45bl,
45ar, 47bl, 64, 65 main, 78, 103.*

Steven Shailer

+ 1 917 518 8001
Pages 55 inset, 63r, 82a, 139a.

Story

4 Wilkes Street
London E1 6QF
020 7377 0313
Story is an ever-changing & evolving lifestyle
gallery/shop located near Brick Lane market.
Part of the Story project is 'Story Deli' – a
must for East End visitors.
*Endpapers, pages 33r, 68–69 (all except 68ar),
86, 100–101, 123.*

Tsé & Tsé associées

Catherine Lévy & Sigolène Prébois
www.tse-tse.com
*Pages 4, 5, 20a, 24bl, 51r, 56 main, 59, 61bl,
66al, 66bc, 70–71, 88–89, 93, 106–107, 121l,
126, 130, 139b.*

index

Page numbers in *italics* refer
to illustrations.

acknowledgments

Emily Chalmers would like to thank everyone who made this book possible, especially Alison Starling, for dreaming up the wonderful project; Gabriella Le Grazie, for getting in touch and directing us in her special way; Emily Westlake, for her support; Paul Tilby, for his graphics skills; and Henrietta Heald and all the hard-working team at Ryland Peters & Small. Ali, thank you once again for your optimism and inspiration; and thank you to all those flea-market fans who allowed us to feature their wonderful homes.

A special thank you goes to the lovely Debi Treloar – my flea-market friend.

Ali Hanan's thanks goes to Henrietta Heald for her thoughtful, sensitive editing; to Alison Starling for asking her to work on such a lovely book; to the vivacious, warm and wonderful Emily Chalmers for her flowers, conversation and inspirational ideas; and to her own in-house team, Dizzy, Luca and tiny Rosa.